DRIVE OF FAITH

The journey of a lifetime

Dr. Russell Kenneth Pier, Jr.

Contents

Dedication

This narrative would have been much, much different if there had been anyone else in my co-pilot's seat during the *Drive of Faith*. The tenacity to stick with me when the going was rough, the commitment to Christ and the vision that came with this *Drive,* and the sacrifices our trip demanded was over and beyond that of the normal Christian.

Doris Estelle Rosen Pier, I could have never made the long trek up this spiritual Appalachian Trail without you by my side for over 59 years. Two thirds of the credit for the success of our *Drive of Faith* belongs to you and you alone. I am so grateful for God's direction in January of 1943 when we fell in love with each other and that August 1 of the same year when we pledged our troth at that altar on Clinton Street, Westfield, NY before the man of God, Pastor Nelson J. Kenyon.

To God be all the glory for arranging our lives and journey together. I am dedicating this book to Doris Estelle Rosen Pier and every dollar of the proceeds from its sale will go into a DORIS E. PIER scholarship fund to provide an education for people who have no way of providing their cost at Faith Bible College International, 29 Main Road, Charleston, ME 04422.

Preface

The Apostle Paul was a pioneer Gospel preacher who touched his generation with a message that changed lives. Stop for a moment and think what our New Testament would look like if he had never picked up a pen. This thought along with serious promptings from relatives and friends moved the juices in my cranium to write this historical volume.

This most earnest prayer involves the reason I wrote, although any reader will find blessing while he peruses along this journey: *Dear Father, touch each line of this manuscript with Your presence, anointing it to challenge the youth of another generation. May some young people that have little to offer be inspired to present themselves at God's altar of sacrifice as a life-long pioneer to preach the holiness message from the Bible.*

The journey begins with the probable prayers of my forefathers. There is no proof of that, but I am assuming from hints of our history there were those that prayed. If not, I can certainly write that my mother's private dedication of her firstborn son establishes a starting point.

Information from my nephew, Kelvin Pier (my brother, Milton's youngest son) was very helpful in documenting some of the family history. My sister Ruth and other siblings contributed bits and fragments along with a personal conversation with Aunt Betty, my mother's youngest sister. I regret that I did not get more information from my grandparents and parents while they were alive. Biographies that could have been written by my uncles, aunts, grandparents, etc. would have been so helpful. I trust this book will help future generations and inspire my siblings to write family history for the same reason.

The *Drive of Faith* begins with my prenatal history and follows my years to the present, 2020. There have been over 10 years of laborious efforts to produce this volume. There are many places I wish were different, but what I have written is as accurate as my memory allows. Some may feel that their life has been so pure every thought and action could be put in their autobiography. I cannot do that; I had sins to repent of that I don't want in this book or any other publication. You need to know that you are not reading a book from a holy angel, but from a human being of Adam's race who was subject to the same temptations that you face. And he did not always win.

Acknowledgements

To Dawn Coffin, MLS, DD
for the hours of extraordinary
effort she spent in editing this material.

To my friend, David Lehr,
who arranged the text for computer printing
and had it published for me.

To my daughter, Rev. Dorene Pier Royal
who designed the front cover.

Introduction

Prepare your brain as you begin reading a story that could challenge what you do with the rest of your days on earth. It begins with the believable presumption of prenatal prayers and ends after nearly 100 years of my life. Please notice the vital parts of this biography. Mother dedicates her first born son to God. I am converted in my pre-teen years. Two godly pastors mentor and encourage an early Bible college education. An exceptional young lady becomes part of my life for 60 years. Challenging Ministerial opportunities are met with prayer and tenacious resolution in places where it looked impossible. Last but not least, retirement has never been considered; there is always something to do for lost souls if you really care.

May this saga from the cradle to the rapture (or the grave, whichever comes first) be helpful to a reader who wants their entire life to count the most for eternity.

Chapter 1

In the Beginning

The Red Coats had come and musketeers were blasting away as civil unrest filled Europe and spilled over into the British Isles in the mid-seventeenth century. It was amid this turmoil that Thomas Pier began to breathe the air of this earth. There is no record of his early life but in 1673 he wooed Mary Witherstone and they were wed in Worcestershire, England. Five years later we read of them again when their first child was born in the New World. Her birth was recorded in the clerk's office at Lyme, CT, as Sarah Pier. It is left up to you to imagine what could have caused these newlyweds to set sail for America and settle in Connecticut.

We may properly assume that Tom and Mary had a Christian background. They both carried Bible names as did their offspring for several generations. Their first boy was dubbed Thomas Jr. who became the father of Thomas III. Levi, Reuben, and Silas were the next three generations. Silas was my great grandfather. Silas named one of his sons William Henry, who was the father of my dad, Russell Kenneth. None of these knew of the *Drive of Faith,* but were very much a part of the one God chose nearly three hundred years later to steer this ship.

It may be wild speculation, but I have lived for years under the assumption that my English forefathers prayed for their progeny. Perhaps some of them read the words of Isaiah 59 (KJV) and claimed it for their own;

> *"As for me, this is my covenant with them, saith the LORD;*
> *My spirit that is upon thee, and my words which I have put*
> *in thy mouth, shall not depart out of thy mouth, nor out of the*

*mouth of thy seed, nor out of the mouth of thy seed's seed,
saith the LORD, from henceforth and forever."*

What better reason do we have that eight offspring of a poor farmer in western New York State were saved, filled with the Spirit with the sign evidence of speaking in tongues; all five boys became preachers and their three sisters became teachers of the Word during their lifetime. All eight have been at some time or other an integral part of this Drive of Faith.

The assumption also has credence when we consider that a boy like me without natural talent in the *fine arts* was chosen to be the author of this *Drive of Faith* before he was born in the middle 20s of the last century. Here is a kid of 17 who found it like self-murder to stand before his high school class and give a book report. To sit in a leadership chair was out of the question. And yet, God formed him in the womb with the right temperament and aptitude for a pioneer in his field and led him in strange paths to finally use him in this *Drive of Faith*. We have to contribute it all to the grace of God. May readers find encouragement and help in this story of faith.

I should say something about my maternal grandparents and their faith in God. Omri Jared and Daisy Elva Wentworth Hunter were the parents of my mother, Helen Laverne Hunter. Little is known of my maternal grandfather's lineage except what my Uncle Bob (granddad's son) told us when I was a young lad. He researched and discovered his father was a descendant of Henry Hudson, the first European to discover the Hudson River. I do not know if Uncle Bob had any documentation for his findings. I do know that Grandfather attended the Methodist Church in Ripley, NY, and I went with him a number of times. I also remember the following little anecdote:

> *Mr. Grover's farm was near my grandfather's. I knew Mr. Grover because his daughter, Betty, was in my class at school. One Lord's Day morning Mr. Grover was hooking up his team to a plow, ready to prepare his garden. Grandad spoke to Mr. Grover and warned him that his plow could break as he was desecrating the Lord's Day. Mr. Grover*

laughed it off and proceeded to plow the land. Grandfather went back to his favorite chair on the porch and watched as his neighbor plowed. Within the hour, Mr. Grover's plow hit a large boulder breaking the blade on the plow.

Our Nana Hunter's father was a podiatrist whose surname was Wentworth. Nana was very much a straight laced English lady who wanted everything just right. She knew her manners and wanted to be sure her grandchildren had an education in the same. She was making breakfast one morning while Granddad was in the barn doing chores. The iron skillet was warming up on the kitchen stove as she laid the pieces of bacon on it. As she did, I was figuring how many pieces each person would get; there was Granddad, Nana, Uncle Bob, Aunt Betty, and myself (I was about 6 or 7). When Nana saw what I was doing, it did not take her long to let me know that was improper and she gave me a good scolding. It was a lesson in this *Drive of Faith* that has lasted me a life time; what others have should not be my concern; God gives to one and takes away from another and what He does is none of my business. Nana was very particular about my shoes being shined and my hair combed when I left for school. She taught me many manners that have helped me during this *Drive of Faith*.

Labor Day was special for my parents in 1924. My mother, Helen Laverne Hunter, was working for Cleo Pier and was invited to stay for the Labor Day celebrations at their home. I do not know, but I suspect that Cleo was playing cupid as she introduced Helen to her brother-in-law, Russell Kenneth. Helen had a date with a young man that night but she canceled it after meeting the man who became my father. Helen never lacked for dates but dates were seldom repeated as she would not allow them to touch her or even kiss her. It was love at first sight with Russell and Helen, and in less than 3 full months they were married on November 29, 1924. I do not know when they took their first kiss, but from my earliest memory, my mom and dad were kissing buddies; he never left the door of our home or returned from the chores without taking mom in his arms and kissing her. They were examples to me when I entered this *Drive of Faith;* Doris and I were kissing buddies all our married lives.

Mother lived in New York State where the law required both parties to be over 21 for marriage. My dad was a farmer and Nana would have never signed for her daughter, Helen, to marry anyone below her caliber. As a result and with the help of Irwin and Betty Weaver, Russell and Helen eloped and were married in Pennsylvania where a license could be obtained legally at 18. They were married by Pastor Frye in Erie and I have their original signed marriage license in my file. They stayed that night at the Weavers.

The next day they showed up at Granddad and Nana's place in Ripley, NY. My dad was carrying his new wife in his arms from the vehicle to the house because she did not have any boots for her feet. Nana was fit to be tied at these actions until they told her they were married. This was the first time they had met Russell, a handsome brute with big dimples; in fact one of his nicknames was *Dimples*. I would like to know the rest of the story, but I am afraid we must all wait until they can share it with us in eternity. They lived with friends or relatives until they could find their own rent. Ten months and thirteen days after they said *I do*, a baby boy with black curly hair, weighing eight and one-half pounds, was born on Main Street in the town of North East, Pennsylvania. Dr. Hurd was the physician who attended my mother in their home; he was the same doctor who brought my father into the world twenty two and one-half years earlier. That boy was destined to become the one who would take this chariot down the road as the *Drive of Faith*.

Supposition says it was mother who named me after my father, giving me the initials for Junior at the end of my name. Mother was brought up in the Methodist church but neither of my parents was religious at the time of my birth. Strangely, mother did something unusual for a sinner. One day, while sitting alone, she held me up in her arms and hands and said a prayer something like this: *"Dear God, this is my first born son. I read somewhere in the Bible that you asked mothers to give their first born sons to you. Here he is, he is all yours. In Jesus name, Amen."* Little did mother know that I would be the first in the family to receive Christ as my Savior, the first to attend Bible College, the first to become a preacher of the Gospel, and the first to become a professor in a Bible College. Her short prayer as a sinner had a lot to do with the *Drive of Faith* in my life.

Russell Kenneth Pier, Sr.

Helen Laverne Hunter

Chapter 2

Pre-school Years

The memories of my early childhood are limited, but I will cite some incidents that I think might be related to the *Drive of Faith.* Sixteen months and sixteen days after my birth our family was presented a baby girl who was given the names of Ruth Helen; after my father's sister, Ruth, and Helen, after my mother. Ruth and I became the best of pals and have had a special relationship during our lifetime. She was a blessing to this *Drive of Faith* for more than 20 years. Her entrance into the family caused me to realize an important lesson; for 16 months I had the full attention of both my parents. Now things were different, someone else was here and I felt forgotten. How valuable to learn in our *Drive of Faith* that there are others in our personal world that have greater needs than little 'ole us.

The earliest recollection I have of Ruth is February 13, 1929, when our brother, Milton Lloyd, was born. We had neighbors who were special friends of our parents; so close that we were taught to call them, Uncle Andy and Aunt Julie. It was customary that all of us children be removed from the home when mother was giving birth. On the day mentioned above, daddy dressed us warm and took me and Ruth outdoors. Between our house and Aunt Julie's was a grape vineyard with the rows running straight from our driveway to our neighbors home. If my memory serves me correctly, it was about 100 yards from our house to theirs. Daddy hollered to Aunt Julie who came and waited at the end of the grape row as I took my two year old sister by the hand and we walked over to the neighbors; there was a smidgeon of snow on the ground. I learned at an early age how important it was during life to help those younger and in need; a valuable lesson for the *Drive of Faith.*

At the home where Milton was born, I remember the foxes (daddy ran a fox farm for a rancher) as they ran back and forth in their pens. Dad had to buy up old horses that had seen their day; then shoot them and feed them to the foxes. Mother loved horses and could not stand to hear the shots, so dad would come in the house and tell her when the shooting was to take place. I remember the kitchen was just inside the back door; it had a window that looked down on the fox pens and under the window was an iron sink with a pump on one end where we got our water. It was there in the kitchen that I watched my pregnant mother hold her ears as the shots rang out; when Milton was born, he was stone deaf and lived his whole life without hearing. The following happened when Milton was about nine or ten years old.

This happened a year or two after mother and daddy were saved. Milton had gone to a deaf school in Rochester, NY. He came home for Christmas vacation and attended the Assembly of God where we were saved and where we worshipped. Pastor Terry wanted to pray for Milton's hearing, so he called on my parents to bring him up to the altar. Pastor called for the elders of the church to come and lay hands on Milton as he anointed him with oil. That was a glorious morning as the church shouted when Milton received partial hearing. Sister Essie Oaks, wife of an elder, was moved on by the Holy Spirit to go up and pray with the elders for Milton's ears, but she disobeyed and held to her seat (she told us later).

When Sister Oaks found out he only received partial hearing, she felt terrible and knew that if she had obeyed, Milton may have received complete deliverance. When Milton returned to deaf school, he was tested and to the amazement of the administration he had 25% hearing in one ear and 35% in the other. They contacted my parents and wanted to know what happened when he was home on vacation that changed his hearing. The school declared and his record showed that he was stone deaf when he entered the school originally. Sister Oaks blamed herself for disobeying and felt bad about it for some time. This story has helped me greatly in the *Drive of Faith*; if one disobeys God it can hurt others besides himself.

My brother, Milton Lloyd, was a challenge to my faith and a blessing to my life for many years. We slept together when we were boys; I remember this little incident when I was 7 and he was 4.

It was in the house where our brother Wentworth was born; we had no electric or running water. Milton and I slept together in a room upstairs. On this particular night the moon was shining bright enough that it gave some small illumination to the room. We decided that night to have a pillow fight. We were laughing and clowning around on the bed with pillows going back and forth when we should have been sleeping. I had a pillow up over my head ready to throw at Milton when someone struck a match in the doorway behind me. Both of us turned to see our father on his way to the bed; needless to say, there were two warm bottoms and no more pillow fights that night.

Milton taught me the deaf alphabet so I could communicate with the deaf when needed. He worked with me in the college for many years. When he attended Zion Bible College, he often spent his vacations with us in our home. Milton became a pastor for various deaf churches during his life and taught Sign Language in our college for many years. Several of his students became proficient enough in the language to become interpreters in courts and churches. He was another lesson in the Drive of Faith; sometimes God has bigger plans for us with our handicaps than could have been accomplished if healing had been given.

It was a cool day in November when William Arthur arrived at our house to begin life in 1930. We lived in a country school building that had been renovated into a home for rent. It sat on a country road that led off from the south side of Route 20 in Girard, Pennsylvania. It was early in the morning when my sister Ruth and I, both dressed in those pajamas that kept our feet warm, appeared in the living room to see our new baby brother. Ruth, not quite 4 years old, began to cry. She already had two brothers and it was time for a sister and she let the family know with real tears. Bill, as his nickname became, had red hair much the color of Granddad Pier's. My sister and I both had black hair and the third child, Milton, had brown; so Bill's hair was different and has always been a point admiration by many who knew him.

Many things happened while we lived in that renovated school house; so many I cannot reiterate them all here. My mother drove into the ditch trying to focus on our driveway during her attempt at learning how to drive. She gave up trying to drive after that and would not drive for the rest of her life.

It was on the hilly back yard of that home Ruth and I had fun using our sleds. Boy that I was, relishing the opportunity to tease my sister, I would slide downhill right behind her, then run back up to the top so I could sled down again while she was walking slowly up. It scared the daylights out of her when she saw me coming directly at her. She stood there screaming as I turned quickly aside laughing. I did that until one time I did not turn quick enough and my nose bridge caught the corner of her sled causing blood to flow profusely down my face. I still bear the scar of that escapade. Mother tried to wash and care for the wound while she sent my sister Ruth down the road to get my dad. Ruth stopped at a neighbor's house to visit for some time and never did get to daddy.

Daddy and his brother, Howard, managed a dairy farm where we lived when Bill was born. I spent much of my time down at the farm, learning many things that have helped me in my *Drive of Faith*. Besides teasing my sister with the sled, I had the feeling I could do most anything I attempted. It was there, at 5 years of age, I got in the panel truck with my cousin Junior (Uncle Howard's oldest) and backed it out of the drive and started down the road. My mother thought my dad was going into town and she needed some groceries so she came out on the porch and hollered *Russell, wait a minute.* She could not tell it was me driving and my name is the same as my dad's. So I stopped the vehicle, put it in reverse, backed up the road just a few yards, and drove it back into the drive. I don't remember now, but I am sure I had a hard time sitting in a chair that day.

It was in the back yard of that farm where Junior, Ruth, and I, were sitting on the top rail of a wooden fence surrounding a barnyard. There were a dozen or so sheep grazing casually on the other side of the fence. I dared my cousin or Ruth to get in with the sheep and pet the face of the male buck. They refused but dared me to do it. Adventurist and risky that I am, I said,

Sure. Down off the fence I got and walked softly and slowly over to the buck, reached down and petted the front of his face, turned around and looked up at cousin and sister, and said, *see there, nothing to it.* I walked back to the fence and just as I got to it something powerful hit me in the seat of my pants. In split seconds I found myself sitting on the ground on the other side of the fence. The hurt did not bother me like the scare and I started to bawl.

My father was coming out of the house and saw it all happen; he made one leap over the fence and grabbed that buck's right ear and took off with it across the barnyard. I do not remember what happened the rest of the day, but, needless to say, I have not tried petting a buck sheep since 1930. The daring spirit I had, even though I sometimes used it for the wrong purpose, inspired me over my life time as I carried on the *Drive of Faith* to perform the will of God.

Russell, Jr., Milton, Ruth

Russell Jr. and Ruth Helen

Chapter 3

1931 to 1933

Sometime in the summer of 1931 our family left the farm where Bill was born and moved to South State Street in Ripley, NY. I am estimating the house was about one half mile from the center of town and the school I was to attend. It was a two story cream colored house that sat back about 30 feet from the sidewalk on the west side of the street. Daddy hung an old tire with a rope from a large maple branch on the tree in the front yard. Ruthie and I had a lot of fun swinging on that old tire; what I did not realize was the bond we were creating between the two of us. It would bring us back together nearly forty years later at Faith School of Theology in Brooklin, ME. Ruth and I worked together for over twenty years in the *Drive of Faith.*

Mother walked me to school the first day. My first grade teacher was Miss Hall, a blond haired lady of average height, approximately 30 years of age. Mother must have talked with Miss Hall about how affectionate our family was; we never went to bed or outdoors to play without kissing mother. Miss Hall kissed me goodbye every day before I left school. She told me she was going to wait for me to grow up, but I doubt if she is somewhere still waiting. The fundamentals in education I learned in her class have been a great blessing through the years; I am so glad she taught me phonetics.

Something happened in my first grade at school that embarrasses me to write about. However, there is an illustration in it that may help people know when we mess up our lives we need to take care of it directly. It is possible in a life of faith to presume rather than believe; we must know the will of God before believing for results otherwise we may end up presuming and be embarrassed. Throughout my younger life, I had some difficulties with control. As a result, I found myself sitting in class with an odor I didn't like. It soon filled the room and the teacher went from student to student to find out where it was coming from. When she came to me, she said kindly, *Russell, I think you better go home for the afternoon.*

It didn't take me long to leave and head for home. I don't know if mother's smeller was working that day or not but she did wonder why I was home from school a little earlier than usual. It must have been a cool day as when daddy came home from work, he stoked the furnace down cellar; a furnace that had one three foot square register in the middle of the living room. We children were all playing around the register when suddenly daddy, who was reading the paper said, *Helen, something smells in here.* Mother was getting supper but she stopped long enough to come in the living room where we were and it did not take her long before she was dragging me off to the bathroom. She washed me real good and gave me a change of clothes; needless to say, that was the last and only time I made such a mess. In your *Drive for Faith,* take care of messes when they happen before the rest of God's family has a chance to know about it.

By the time I entered second grade, we had moved to another home on Hillside Road in Ripley. The home was located nine tenths of a mile from the school; the school bus could not pick you up unless you lived a full mile or more. This made it necessary for me to walk to school every day. Those who know the kind of snowstorms coming off Lake Erie (two miles north of our home) during the winter can imagine the struggle a little seven year old boy had during the cold months. There was no electric in that house, so I did homework via kerosene lamps.

We had a washing machine that ran with human muscle by a handle on the side that went round and round. Every Saturday morning, I was the human muscle in the little wash room. Around, around, around, and around; I never did count the number it took to wash a tub of clothes but it seemed like millions (at least to a little boy). I learned a life lesson; when one lacks the equipment and money to buy such, you make do with what you have. That was another helpful lesson preparing me for the *Drive of Faith.*

It was in that home that my next brother was born. Dr. Parsons came from down in the town and we children were scuttled across the street to Devillo Hubbard's (one of my classmates) house. My baby brother, Wentworth Lavern, arrived on time. Who would have thought he would be one of the charter members I asked to serve on the Board of Directors of F.S.T. 26 years later? All of my brothers and sisters have served with me in various capacities in the *Drive of Faith* at the Faith School of Theology.

An interesting part of Wentworth's life took place in the summer of 1951. He worked on a farm near my parent's home in Western Pennsylvania. He had backslid and was not serving the Lord. That summer I was visiting my parents and had a chance to talk with Wentworth. The day I started on my trip back to Maine, I felt to drive by the farm where he was working. I saw him sitting under an apple tree eating his lunch; I rolled down the window of my '36 Plymouth and hollered, *"See you in Bible school this fall"*. He laughed and thought that was the biggest joke he had ever heard.

In a few days after I had arrived home in Maine, I had a call from Pennsylvania. It was none other than Wentworth asking if he could come and stay with us until he could find a job. We gave him the thumbs up, and to make a longer story shorter, he got reclaimed and that September registered as a freshman in Zion Bible Institute. He graduated in 1954, married a beautiful young lady who attended our church, and was in the ministry his whole life until retiring and passing to his eternal reward at age 81. The prophetic word of knowledge is helpful in the life of one devoted to a *Drive of Faith.*

Many memories linger in my mind from the year we lived on the Hillside Road. My father raised a couple of pigs, butchered them himself, and smoked the bacon. I thought it would be nice to wear glasses, so I faked my eye test at school and was fitted with a pair. I threw a stone at my brother, Milton (less than 4 years old), to land near him in the grass and startle him; to my chagrin, it landed on the side of his head leaving a large gash and a scar he bore the rest of his life. Needless to say, I felt terrible and never threw stones to land near anyone the remainder of my life.

Drive of Faith

I walked a mile from that Hillside home past a cemetery to buy 2 quarts of raw milk for the family at $.05 a quart from Farmer Engles each evening. My neighbors were Devillo Hubbard, Francis Eimers, and Helen Munson; all in my class of second grade. My teacher was Mrs. Smith. She must have talked to Miss Hall from the first grade as she kissed me goodbye every Friday when I left school.

An embarrassing moment happened in my second grade gym class. Wally Johnson, the gym teacher, always lined us up in the gymnasium in cold weather according to our height. Then he would call off our names and we would answer. On my left was a girl by the name of Patricia Hammond. She reached up and kissed me on the cheek just as the teacher looked up. I heard the teacher say, *Well, Russell* – I cannot remember what else he said but the whole class looked down the line to see what happened. Needless to say, that is probably the only time in my life that I turned red in the face. I learned that day something that has helped me in this *Drive of Faith;* expect the unexpected most anytime and do not be surprised if it embarrasses you.

It was at this home my father came home drunk (the only time in my life that I remember). His friend, Red, drove him home in an ancient pickup and before dad got out of the car he reached over and bit Red on the nose; why I never found out. He brought the groceries in from the pickup and mother was upset when she saw that he bought a whole bag of light bulbs. She asked where they came from. We had a store in town named *The Quality Cash.* Dad said, *I got them at the Squality Squash.* Immediately she knew he was drunk and made him walk the line on the Congoleum. He stumbled and went outdoors to regurgitate. Mother was not happy with him. He lay on the couch as sick as a dog. My sister Ruth (5 years old) was babying him when mother told her to leave her father alone, saying "*he deserves to be sick*". Daddy got drunk from the liquor others bought – he never used family money to drink. There are lots of lessons in this paragraph that have stood by me in this *Drive of Faith.*

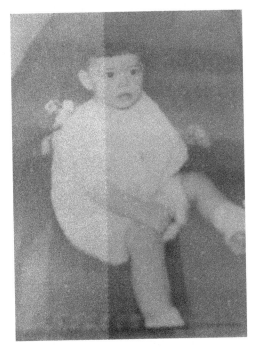

Wentworth Laverne Pier

Chapter 4

1933 to 1935

The next year after Hillside Road we moved to Academy Street in Ripley about a block from the school yard. I have many pleasant memories at that house. It was at this house my siblings and I had whooping cough. I remember laying in my stomach on the front lawn and whooping.

In the evening when daddy was away at work on the night shift, we children sat on the front porch in a family swing with mother. She would send one of us to the store to buy fudgesicles. When they arrived we hurried to eat them because every once in a while the stick would say *"free"* and we could take it to the store and collect another one. There was a cherry tree we enjoyed climbing in the side yard and a sandbox in the rear of the house. Our neighbor was a widow by the name of Mrs. Borman. I slept all winter on a screened in porch (second floor) with my brother Milton. He and I played games under the quilts to keep warm.

Neither of my parents was saved so my mother had a chance to get her fortune told while we lived in that home. Among other things the soothsayer said, *"Helen, this Saturday a dog will come to your place and you will have a difficult time getting rid of it"*. Sure enough, that next Saturday a large German Shepherd appeared in our yard. We kids loved it, named it *Bozo,* and played with it for hours until dad came home that night. My daddy would never allow an animal to suffer and he knew we did not have food enough to feed the family, let alone a large dog. As soon as he could, daddy took the dog to the dog pound and had him locked up under the keepers care. He broke loose at least two times and each time showed up in our yard; we had a difficult time getting rid of him. In our *Drive of Faith* we need to understand that the devil's imps may create situations that appear to those around us to be just fine, but to those who walk in the Sprit it is known as the work of the enemy. Because of the company around us and their love for the carnal, we may have a difficult time exposing the work of the enemy and freeing our yard from his presence.

It was a cool day in the fall of 1934 in Ripley. I was on my way home from school when I saw my father with a team of horses and a wagon full of furniture. He was on his way to our new home on Wattlesburg Hill. I hurried to the house and asked my mother if I could run after daddy and go with him on the wagon to our new home. She agreed and I took off up the street, but by this time they had gotten out of sight far ahead. I knew the general direction and even though the trip was three miles long, I kept walking. By the time I got there the men had the wagon unloaded. Nevertheless, I had a chance to see the house and buildings on the property where we would live and enjoyed riding back to town with my dad. I had walked up the three mile hill to experience the blessing of being with my hero, my dad. Often in this *Drive of Faith* I have had similar circumstances where God asked me to do what I could do to climb a hill; then He would bless me with an easier trip back to my work for His Kingdom.

There are many memories living there on Wattlesburg Hill. There was a large empty barn where we children kept our make-believe horses that were simply four foot long saplings. Some were white birch, some dark cherry, etc. We tied a piece of clothes line around one end and ran around the vacant farm with these between our legs as if they were horses. We had a black Belgian police dog that relatives had sent us. We named him Rex; he protected the family tenaciously. We bought milk daily from the Gliddens who lived next door. The water pump was in the barn some distance from the house. Since I was the oldest boy, I was elected to carry pails of water for the family each day.

The highway passing our house got covered with ice during the winter. We had a lot of fun on our sleds sliding for a half a mile or more. Ruth and I attended a one-room school house where our dear teacher taught all eight grades. I would estimate that there were between 18 and 25 students, as I remember. An under classman could learn as much as he wanted by listening in on the lesson given to the class up front. At that one room country school house I learned the value of self-education as I listened to upperclassmen receiving their lessons; this has helped me in my *Drive of Faith*. It was here I learned how to play "Anti-anti-over" as we threw a tennis ball over the roof of the school building. Teams were chosen and we never knew exactly where the ball would come when the other team threw it. In the *Drive of Faith* that little game taught me to expect the unexpected and be prepared to react quickly.

One more important lesson was learned while living on Wattlesburg Hill. Less than a mile from our home was a country gas station where the blind owner sold gas and kerosene oil. My dad taught me to never take advantage of the handicapped. Daddy told me how some people had tried to give the blind man a one dollar bill, claiming that it was a five or ten. I thought how terrible that was and have never forgotten it in my *Drive of Faith*. Many times it has helped me to reach out to the poor and needy and give them a free education at our Bible College.

My second sister, Pamela Daisy, was born on April 11, 1935, while we lived on Wattlesburg Hill. Sometime in the fall of that year the family moved to a large home in Forsythe, NY, a small community between Ripley and Westfield on Route 20. Ruth and I attended another one room brick school of five grades. The house sat back about 40 feet from Route 20, a major highway between Buffalo and Chicago. That winter we witnessed a devastating snow storm that closed Route 20 from Buffalo to Erie, PA. That morning I was appointed to dig a tunnel between the house and the outhouse as there was a drift at least 8 feet high; my brothers and sister needed to use the two-hole facility.

Pamela Daisy Pier

Chapter 5

Something Good and Something Bad

This was the home where our Christian salvation began. It was a bright Sunday morning in the fall of 1935 that found my sister Ruth and us three boys playing in our bare feet in the dirt drive way. Brother Frank Davidson and his wife, neighbors up the road, drove in our yard in their large Buick car. Their first words were, *"Would you children like to go to Sunday School?"* Fortunately, none of us hated school and this sounded great; get to ride in a big Buick and travel some place for an education.

I ran to the back porch and into the kitchen. My mother was busy at the old iron sink by the window. She could see the car drive in where we were playing. I said excitedly, *"Mom, they want us to go to Sunday School; can we, please?"* Mother shook her head no, looking at our bare feet and play clothes. She told us kindly that we were not dressed for such an occasion. She went to the car and talked with the Davidsons, explaining that if they would stop next Sunday, she would have us ready. That next Sunday was a day that changed this family for eternity; it will never be forgotten in this *Drive of Faith.*

It was at this home that daddy made some homemade brew (beer). It wasn't more than two quarts and he lowered it into the cold well water in a container to get chilled. He never got drunk on it and I do not remember him making it more than once. I don't think my mom was pleased about it but neither was it a point of contention between them. He gave me a small sip of it; it is the only time in my life I have ever even tasted beer or wine. I dread to think what could have happened to my life, along with my brothers, if Jesus had not come to our home; that year to us children, and two years later to our parents.

It was that next Sunday in October of 1935 that Ruth and I rode in that big Buick to the Assembly of God. It was located in a hall above Kingan's Drug Store on the Main Street of Westfield, NY. Rev. Theodore Terry was the pastor and Gerald Oaks was the Sunday School Superintendent. My sister and I were shown the way to the children's hall where they sang and were dismissed to their classes. I went with about six boys my age to a wide open attic where there were 8 or 10 chairs sitting in a circle. Ida Oaks accompanied us as our teacher. She sat down and took out her book, taking the attendance. She put my name down as a new comer and then turned to ask me a simple question I shall never forget; *"Russell, wouldn't you like to let Jesus into your heart?"* I did not know much about Jesus, but I knew He was a good man. I said *"Yes"*, as I knelt by my chair amidst a couple of snickers from the boys. I repeated after my teacher the simple words asking Jesus to forgive my sins and come into my heart. That was one of the happiest days of my life. It was really the beginning of a personal *Drive of Faith* for this young lad.

I do not remember what the church service was like, but when I arrived home and jumped out of that big Buick, I ran in the house. Mother was at the sink, just inside the door by the window. I excitedly said, *"Mom! I asked Jesus into my heart today!"*. Her rather nonchalant answer was, *"well, that's nice"*. The Davidsons picked us up each Sunday after that and I was able to build a Bible foundation in that small church that has been with me throughout my life in this *Drive of Faith*.

Our introduction to the Assembly of God was a life changing moment for the family. Pastor Theodore Terry was a compassionate man of God who instilled in us the Word of the Lord. He was a man of faith. In those days it was necessary to have a quarantine sign on the door of your home if you had certain communicable diseases. The town doctor had come to know Pastor Terry. On one occasion the doctor came to quarantine the Terry home; his words to our pastor were, *"I would leave you these pills for this sickness but I know as soon as I leave you would flush them down the toilet"*. He was known as a *man of faith* and he taught us all how to trust in God. That was 80 years ago. I still remember the faith truth he preached about mountains, mustard seeds, and believing God for anything you needed. It worked for our family then and it still works for many of us today. It impacted my young life with truth that has been with me over the years in this *Drive of Faith*.

Sometime in the early fall of 1936, our family made a fateful move to a second floor apartment on Goodrich Street in Ripley, NY. We rented from a family by the name of *Burdin*. I use the word fateful because that was the place our dear sister Pamela Daisy became a cripple through Infantile Paralysis, better known as Polio. It happened like this; a little boy living in a house on the corner of Goodrich and Main died with Polio. I stood on the sidewalk across the street next to the Baptist Church and watched as men carried out the mattress of the little boy that died. They burned it in their garden spot; a sight I have never forgotten.

The Baptist preacher, who lived across from our house, had a boy about the age of my brother, Bill. The preacher's boy had played with the boy that died and became exposed to Polio. My brother, Bill, played with the preacher's son before anyone realized he had been exposed. As a result, Bill caught the germ which consequently was passed on to all of the children in our family. Many people have had Polio and did not know it; one regurgitates and is sick for one day and it is all over with. We were told it only cripples one in a hundred. Ruth, Milton, Bill, Wentworth, and I had Polio and did not know it until Pam, our baby sister, came down with it.

We were told at that time Pam was the only case they knew of that did not regurgitate. I remember vividly that November (1936) afternoon when I was standing beside my sister Pam in a small room off the parlor. She squatted down on her haunches but could not get back up. Evidently it was hurting and she started to cry. I went and got my mother and told her something was wrong with Pam. The remainder of that afternoon and evening is a blur as I do not remember anything, but the next morning is as clear as a bell.

The children's bedrooms were behind the kitchen which made it necessary for us to walk through the kitchen to get to the parlor. I was alone as I walked into a dark living room. I remember the eerie feeling that came over me when I saw a bed in the living room and my precious baby sister propped with pillows and sand bags by her feet. Daddy had called a doctor from Sherman, NY, during the night. He had diagnosed the condition in my sister's body as Infantile Paralysis. I felt a heavy pall of darkness come over me as I listened to mother tell me about Pam. We were all quarantined and missed a couple of weeks or more of school.

The following is another episode that happened on Goodrich Street that influenced my faith in this journey. Both of my siblings, Ruth and Bill, developed double pneumonia. The doctor who came to our home late in the day told my parents that they would both have to be taken to the hospital in the morning if they were not better. That evening Pastor Terry and a deacon came to anoint and pray for both sick ones. My parents were unsaved but welcomed their prayers. When the doctor came next morning, he was amazed to find them so much improved and wondered what happened. This influenced my parents and remained in my memory to inspire me in this *Drive of Faith.*

At some time following her initial development of Polio, my sister Pam was taken to a specialized hospital by the title, Buffalo Children's Guild. She lay for two years at BCG on a stiff board. We have her picture from the front page of the Buffalo News with dolls all around her. She was a beautiful child with long curls; the caption in the news read, *A Doll Among Dolls.* It was a very trying time, better than two years, for both Pam and her parents. They had no vehicle and could only depend on Pastor Terry and our Aunt Cleo for transportation over the 50 miles to Buffalo. Pam was blessed to have our Aunt Betty living near Buffalo who visited her quite often. She was four years old when she returned home from the Guild. My sister, Pam, was an inspiration to me and has been throughout this *Drive of Faith.* I have learned from her; when God does not do what you want and what you think He should, you keep right on serving Him for He has other plans you know nothing about.

One more thought about my sister, Pam, the girl with braces on her legs for several years. My father had a way of teaching his children that there was nothing they could not accomplish if they set their mind to it. If one of us should say, *"I can't make this work",* or *"I can't do this";* my dad would ask, *"How do you spell our name?"* Then, of course we would say, *"P I E R"*. Immediately he would add, *"Don't you ever forget that a Pier never says, I can't"*. My sister, Pam, took that to heart as we all did. She would climb trees with braces on both legs, and one time I had to get a ladder and get her down from a roof where she had climbed. This philosophy has blessed me well in the many years of this *Drive of Faith.*

Main Street Looking East, Westfield, N. Y.

Chapter 6

The Beginning of a Christian Home

Sometime early in the year 1937, the family moved to North State Street in Ripley where our baby sister, Mary Jane, was born. Previous to her birth on July 18, my parents were saved. It happened like this; one evening when all the children were in bed except me, Pastor Terry and Deacon Davidson came as invited to our humble home. We met in the small living room. I sat on a day bed in the corner to the right as you walked through the archway from the dining room. Pastor and deacon sat in front of me facing my parents who sat on the left. The pastor got out his guitar and began to sing with the deacon some of the old songs of the church.

My dad was simply crazy over guitar music and enjoyed every syllable as it was sung. After a few songs, Pastor explained the way of salvation to my parents. We all knelt by our chairs; mom by her wicker and daddy by his blue leather rocker. I do not know what they said, nor whether or not it was verbal, but I remember mother saying when she rose to her feet, *I saw a bright light;* and when she did her sins were gone. Daddy said, *"I felt like a huge burden rolled off my back".*

From that day on, things were different in our home. Mother and Dad started family prayers, teaching every one of us the importance of daily devotions. As soon as daddy got a vehicle, we never missed a service at church; even revival meetings that lasted for 6 weeks. The first car dad bought was a 1928 two-door Chevrolet and the second was a 1929 Model A Ford. Both cars seemed to last forever, perhaps because they spent so much time going to and from church services.

A cute little incident happened at this house, with a glassed in front porch, where Mary was born. Our four year old brother, Wentworth, better known in those days as Buster, was playing in the yard one day with the neighbor children. He stood up on either a tree stump or box of some type, and started preaching to the kids that had gathered. During his preaching, he purposely fell over on the ground. He told the children that this was what his pastor (Rev. Terry) did when he was preaching. He had seen Pastor fall under the anointing of the Holy Spirit and lay prostrate on the platform. Those were days on this *Drive of Faith* that blessed us, growing up under old fashioned Holy Ghost teaching and demonstrations of the Spirit.

During our stay in the home where dad and mother were saved, I had an interesting experience at school. I was eleven years old and in sixth grade at the Ripley Elementary School. We had a real bully in our class that liked to throw his weight around and get attention. I remember his name well but will not use it here for obvious reasons. He would show off by swinging in the school swings so fast and high that his swing would go clear over the rail that held the swings. One afternoon just before class was getting out, he got permission to go down stairs to the boys room. When he came back up the stairs, class had already been dismissed and we were all going down the stairs. As he was coming up, he would take his shoulder and push each classmate, just to show off. I was about the fourth or fifth one and I prepared to meet him with my shoulder. When he came to me, he started his maneuver and I let him have it with my shoulder and knocked him over.

This was out of character for me as I never got into fights at school. After I pushed him, I grabbed the rail and catapulted over, dropping about eight feet to the floor below and took off running out the door and down the street. I knew I did not have time to make it across the school yard to my own home, so I made a path to my grandparent's home. The bully came after me with about four or five boys who wanted to see the fun. I ran up on the porch and there was a note on the door that made my heart sink, The note was from my nana who wrote; "*Gone to Helen's*". The bully saw the note and started slowly up the stairs, chiding me with, "*Ah, ha, ha; nobody home.*"

I did not know that my Grandfather (a big man over 6 feet tall) worked nights and was sleeping. He heard the commotion and opened the door just as the bully was taking the last step. Granddad made a B line to the bully and just missed grabbing his hair. Granddad said, *"If I had got your hair boy, I would have pulled it out from the roots"*. Obviously he said some other things to the bully that I do not remember, but the boys and bully all left in quick fashion. I have used this story on several occasions to illustrate how you can trust a big God that loves you, arriving on the scene when the devil has you backed into the corner. This story has been another in my *Drive of Faith* that has stood the test of time.

Not long after my sister, Mary, was born, daddy took a job with a Mrs. Simon on a truck farm located on Route 5, Ripley, NY. The farm had a small beach right on Lake Erie and we enjoyed playing in the cool water after a hot day's work in the fields. We raised truck farm commodities such as tomatoes, corn, cabbage, potatoes, and several other vegetables. Mrs. Simon had a small number of dairy cows, perhaps a dozen as I remember. It was there I learned to milk cows by hand every morning before going to school on the bus. I worked with my dad planting tomatoes and cabbage and working the fields. I did not realize it at the time but I was gaining valuable knowledge in gardening that helped us for several years at the college. We grew several acres of food that sustained us through the cold Maine winters. In the late 1930s God was preparing me for another part of this *Drive of Faith*.

There are three or more things that happened at that farm I want to mention. In the summer my dad had mowed a field of timothy, and he sent me with a team of horses to hitch up the hay rake and proceed to pile the hay in windrows across the field. The rake's tongue was facing the highway. There was a small slope between the rake and the road. After I had positioned the team and hooked the harness to the whippletree on the rake, I put one foot up on the rake's tongue. When I tried to get my other foot up, something happened that scared the horses. The reins were out of reach, one foot up and one foot down, and the horses are down the slope and headed down the road to the barn. I am hopping on one foot and yelling to the horses to stop – *Whoa, Whoa, Whoa.* My dad was by the barn when he heard me and came running out into the middle of the road in the path of the horses. He grabbed their bridles and brought them to a quick stop. This sounds like our God who sees our dilemmas and stops at nothing to protect us from serious danger. This is a story that has helped me in my *Drive of Faith.*

It was in that barn that I had played with matches and a fire got out of control. The building started to fill with smoke. I quickly let the cows out and ran with a pail to the creek from which we carried water. Dad came in time to help me and the fire was quenched. Dad never whipped me for playing with matches; he figured I was smart enough to learn my lesson, and I did.

Down the road from Mrs. Simon there lived a boy who was in my class, only child in a well-to-do family. Several times he invited me to his home to play. I do not know whatever happened to Tom Bryson, but have often wondered as I never told him about Jesus. That same year I had a close friend in our sixth grade class by the name of Earl Barger. One sunny day during school lunch hour, he went to the beach at Lake Erie which was only a short distance. While walking along by the water that day, a huge rock let go from the bank above. It struck Earl on the head and killed him instantly. And I had never told him about my Jesus. The names of these two friends stay with me and have helped me to never pass up an opportunity when it appears to speak of the sacrifice of Christ on Calvary. The major reason I am a preacher today in this *Drive of Faith* is because my old fashioned pastor told me the pitter patter of those feet on the sidewalk of our cities is the sound of people on the road to an endless Hell.

Mary Jane

Chapter 7

Bedbugs and a Run-away

S ometime in the fall of 1938, our family moved to a grey colored home next to the High School on North State Street in Ripley. Mother was heavy with child waiting for the December birth of our youngest brother, Stewart. Mother always examined every house we moved to except this one. Dad looked it over briefly and felt it was just the house we needed. Imagine the horror in my mother's eyes when she discovered on the second day that the house was polluted with bedbugs. Wow!

The vocabulary my mother used is gone from my memory, but she did not lack for words when she expressed herself. Mother could be vociferous but she never swore or used curse words and bad language. I'm sure dad was apologetic; most of the time he was meek and mild with a long fuse.

Our beds were set in coffee cans with an inch or so of kerosene; this kept the bugs from sleeping with us. Early in the next day, we were tearing wall paper off the wall. We older children worked with our parents, scraping and digging until every possible home of the ugly bug was erased. New wallpaper, no doubt bought by the property owner, was pasted on the rooms and we had a brand new house.

Mother wanted all the raspberries, black berries, and dewberries she could get to can for the winter. I was elected to go every morning in the summer to a field about a mile up South State Street and spend the better part of the day picking berries all by myself. This lasted about ten days for this thirteen year old kid. In the first place, he felt rejected out there in a field all alone under the hot sun. *Ten days was enough; I'm just not going to do this anymore!*

Plans were laid that evening. Note was written for Milton to give to mom at supper time the next day. A couple of raw potatoes and a loaf of bread was secretly placed in a small wool blanket and tied. Next morning the window opened on second floor and out went the blanket and food. Milton was given the note and pledged to honor his brother's request. About the time I usually left for the berry field, I stopped at the side of the house to pick up my goods and started walking west on Route 20. I was on my way to Aunt Connie's house in Oil City, PA. She had three or four boys around my age and younger and I knew I would be accepted.

Around ten o'clock I had gotten about four miles out of town when I heard a train going by on the tracks about a quarter of a mile from the highway. A delightful thought began to dance in my brain; those trains are going quite slow; why not get a free ride? Over the field to the tracks and it was not long before a train came meandering by. I grabbed a ladder rung on the side of an empty coal car but could not make it with my baggage in the other hand. I decided to throw the blanket with its goodies up and into the next empty car. The toss was successful so I grabbed a rung on the next car and swung up; I would estimate the speed of the train at about twenty miles per hour. I made it across the precarious division between that car and the next to get to my blanket. I have thought sometimes that I could have slipped easily and landed on the track below and be killed. Someone on this *Drive of Faith* had to be watching this crazy kid on his run-away journey.

Route 89 out of North East, PA, was the direction I wanted. It was coming up after a short five or six mile train ride and I needed to disembark. I climbed down the ladder on the outside of the coal car and prepared myself to jump. The train was moving about the same speed, perhaps a dite bit faster. My long pants were a checkered black and white ripping open at the left knee when I landed on the rocky small bank. The skin broke open but it was just an abrasion. There was some water in a ditch running by; I used it to clean myself up. With my blanket and goodies, I started walking up 89.

It was turning a bit dusk when I considered going over in a nearby field and curling up in my blanket. To my surprise, just then a semi stopped and the driver asked if I needed a ride? I said, *Sure,* and thanked him. We were approaching Union City when he ran out of fuel. He got out a gas can but had to say goodbye to me because the company he was driving for did not allow him to leave anyone with the truck. I thanked him again and started my trek in the dark. For the first time in my life, I decided to put out my thumb and tell those passing by I needed a ride. There was a feeling of rain in the air when two ladies offered me a ride in their rear seat. I climbed in just in time to avoid a rain storm. They asked me where I was going and when I told them Oil City which surprised them as that is where they lived. They asked for the address of my destiny and I told them without hesitation, *605 Bissell Avenue*. The one who was not driving looked around at me with surprise written all over her face. Bissell Avenue was where they lived and 605 was up the street from their home. Was there an angel running away with that crazy teen, or was God simply providing help along the *Drive of Faith* for His growing up boy?

They dropped me off at 605 and proceeded on their way. I saw a light in the window upstairs as I walked up the front steps and knocked on the door. Aunt Connie opened the window and hollered down, *Who's there?* I responded with my name and immediately she asked if my granddad was there? I told her I was all alone and she quickly closed the window after telling me she would be right down. As she opened the front door, I could hear a troupe of boys coming down the stairs. They engulfed me with hugs and waited excitedly as I told them of my journey. Aunt Connie opened the fridge and cupboards and in no time had delicious breakfast on the table.

About fifteen minutes had passed when there was a knock on the door. What I did not know was that one of those ladies in the car was the wife of an Oil City police officer. He was standing at the door when Aunt Connie opened. He did not come in but conversed with her, letting her know there was a three State alarm out to find me. He explained that my mother was sitting at her neighbor's home by the phone. Aunt Connie assured the officer she would call her sister and tell her I was safe at her house. What a relief it brought my mom when her older sister called. My precious mother had been crying for her boy and had asked Mrs. Worcester, our next door neighbor, if she could use her phone to call the police, sending out an alarm. It was after ten at night; mom had been there since Milton gave her the note at supper time.

It was one of the greatest summers I ever had. My cousins let me use one of their bikes and we went swimming in the public pool nearly every day. Wow – no berries in the hot sun, kids my age to play with, bike rides, swimming, and a family that treated me like a king's kid. I must have been there three or four weeks before someone was able to give me a ride back to Ripley. It was my granddad, Aunt Connie's father that arrived with my nana for a visit with their family. I said my goodbyes with hugs all around and thanked the whole family for their kindness.

Remember the story of Jonah, how he ran from God in a boat of fishermen? God used him for the salvation of that whole crew; *Then the men feared the LORD exceedingly, and offered a sacrifice unto the LORD, and made vows*, Jonah 1:16. It was while I was a run-away that summer that I had a heart to heart talk with my cousin, a few months younger than I. He surrendered his heart to God. Little did we know at that time, George Powers, Jr. would die with a tumor in the brain at seventeen. The family was Catholic so it was not difficult to convince my cousin that Jesus died for his sins. I expect to meet him on the other side when my *Drive of Faith* is over.

Chapter 8

My First Teenage Year

My parents were extremely gracious when I returned home after two or three weeks at Aunt Connie's. Mother and daddy hugged me and never raised a voice or hand to punish me for my escapade. I was amazed but it has helped me in this *Drive of Faith* to show mercy on college students in times of discipline.

Living next to the school yard on North State could get eerie after dark if you had to walk to nana's house on Ross Street; Ross Street ran parallel with State. My path was right through the school property. In the late '30s school yards in little towns were not lit up with any kind of light. When mother sent me after dark to nana's for any reason, I would sing to the top of my lungs;

> *I'm gonna sing, I'm gonna shout, I'm gonna sing, I'm gonna shout, Praise the Lord. When the gates swing open wide, I'll be right by Jesus side, I'm gonna sing and I'm gonna shout, Praise the Lord.*

Through life in this *Drive of Faith,* there have been many times I found it helped to sing when everything looked dark.

Another thing that happened at that address took place around noon. I walked out of the back door on my way to the street when two boys, walking up the street, called to me pointing to our house roof and saying excitedly, *"Your house is on fire"!* I laughed at them and was sure they were joking and wanted to make fun of me if I looked up at the roof. I had just come from the kitchen; how could the house be on fire? However, those boys were so insistent, hollering so the neighborhood could hear. When I finally turned to look, I was shocked to see fire coming out of the top of our chimney. I ran in the house and told mother I was running up the street to the firehouse and report it. In a few moments the men with the truck were there and the fire was quenched without any damage. I learned from that experience that I needed to listen to others even when it appeared unbelievable; that was another step of learning in this *Drive of Faith.*

There are four more incidents that took place in that home next to the school yard in Ripley. As a *thirteen old* boy, I had developed a ravenous appetite. My mother could can the most delicious ripe peaches in the old fashioned Mason quart jars that I have ever tasted. They were stored in the cellar that had easy access from outside. After coming home and eating lunch, I would slip down cellar and get a quart jar of those peaches, place them under my jacket and head for the small barn a few steps from the house. On the empty second floor of the barn, I would open those peaches and devour about half of its contents, drinking the sweet juice they were canned in. There was a maple sapling reachable by the open second floor barn window; after a full stomach of peaches, I would grab the top of that sapling and land on school property.

After the last class, about 3:00 PM, I would make my way back to the second floor of the barn, pull out the jar with the remainder of those peaches, and consume them in no time. I could not leave the jar around for evidence, so I used all my might to heave it from the back of the barn over into the garden that belonged to Mr. Winebarger, the elementary school's principal. I don't know what he thought when he found those jars in his garden. This was not an everyday occurrence of mine; probably only did it 3 or 4 times during the year. Mother never knew she lost all those jars until I told her decades later. This story helped me years later to understand the appetite of young men coming to Bible college during this *Drive of Faith.*

It was extremely difficult for my dad to communicate with his sons about the birds and the bees. My mother, realizing I was 13 years old and developing into a young man, felt I needed some counsel. I am trying to be exceptionally careful how I word this as I want little eyes to be able to read my story. Mother contacted her younger brother, my Uncle Bob, and arranged for him to instruct me. I do not remember a word he told me except his closing statement; *"Someday, when you get to be president, you will thank me for this"*. Little did my Uncle know at that point in my life that I would actually be president of anything? He was about 6 years older than his young nephew, and after serving in the US Navy, and graduating from Allegheny State College, he became a professor at a University in San Antonia, TX. This incident did help me to see the need of educating Bible college students in this area of their lives. It has been my privilege to sit with scores of students and listen to their difficulties; offering prayer and counsel about sexual matters in this *Drive of Faith.*

My baby brother was born in this home next to the school on December 24, 1938. He served as a teacher at our college in Maine and Headmaster when we started a college in Baltimore. During the first year of his life he developed a serious case of pneumonia. My mother was a new Pentecostal Christian but had been brought up in the Methodist faith. Her Methodist background made her anxious over Stewart if he died. She called the Methodist preacher in Ripley and had him sprinkle and pray a baptismal prayer over her baby boy. While I do not agree with the baptism of babies, I recognize the concern of my mother for the future of her children. I give both her and daddy thanks for their many hours of prayer that has helped keep all eight of their children walking with God in the journey of this *Drive of Faith.*

It was at this address that I developed into self-starter. Going from door to door, I took magazine subscriptions, delivered them each week and collected their money each month. Then I went from door to door in the summer and worked up a clientele. I offered to mow their lawns – twenty-five or fifty cents. I used their equipment which in those days was simple man-power; no electric or gas mowers. I had one lawn on Saturdays that took several hours for which I received two dollars. I always enjoyed treating myself each week with a Clark candy bar; three chocolate bars of most any kind were ten cents when on sale. It appears that God was developing the self-starting pioneer spirit in me for the future *Drive of Faith.*

One more small, but important incident to mention at this address; mother hung her washing on the line each week. Coach Wally Johnson mentioned her beautiful white clean laundry in his gym class one day. His words were something like this; *"What a sparkling clean white laundry Mrs. Pier hung on her line next door today. It shows that soap and water are cheap enough and no one has to be dirty".* That statement has remained with me over the years in this *Drive of Faith,* causing me to realize two things; use plenty of soap and water to stay clean and even a clean laundry can be a witness of your faith in God.

Stewart Van

Chapter 9

A Lesson on Tithing

It was sometime in the year of 1939 that our family moved from Ripley to Academy Street in Westfield, NY. It may have been because it was closer to our church as we did not have a vehicle. Several things happened on Academy Street that I remember quite well. One concerned the Biblical practice of tithing. Our old fashioned pastor taught us that one of the ways to have God's blessing on our lives was to give God ten percent of our income. I remember when Uncle George and Aunt Cleo or Uncle Ralph and Aunt Florence would visit us they would often give each of us children a dime. A dime at that time would buy two cones of ice cream or three regular chocolate bars. Our parents would remind us that one penny of that dime belonged to God for the Sunday offering. Mother and dad lived by that themselves and as a result we never went hungry one meal even though we were very poor. I think daddy was working at that time for fifty five cents an hour.

The only time I remember my parents deviating from the thought of *tithing* was when we lived there on Academy Street. One week we had so little that one of the boys had to stay home from school because he had no shoes. I remember when we had to cut the cardboard that separated the shredded wheat biscuits into the shape of our shoes and tuck them inside to close the small hole that had worn through the sole.

One of the saints in the church heard that my brother had to miss a day at school because he had no shoes. She told my mother that God would not be displeased if she took some of our family tithes and bought a pair of shoes for him. My parents, being new in the faith, listened to that good woman (she actually did some preaching when needed) and bought shoes so my brother could go to school. That very week, for the first and only time, mother had no food to prepare for us children after breakfast on Saturday. She cooked the oatmeal and served it with toast and milk for our breakfast. The cupboards were bare. There was nothing to feed us until daddy came home from his job as chef on a railroad crew around ten o'clock that night.

The scene that followed breakfast that morning will be forever etched on my memory. As usual, mother read from God's Word and then had all of us kneel for prayer. We prayed, each one taking a turn from the oldest to the youngest. Stewart was 2 ½ years old as the youngest and repeated as mother prayed with him. Then mom lifted her heart to God in true repentance, asking God to forgive her for misusing His tithes for my brother's shoes. She closed with an appeal for God to provide for her little brood so they could have something to eat for lunch and supper.

We had no sooner got up from our knees when we heard a knock at the back door. An Italian farmer down the street asked mom if she had a boy old enough to help him. I suppose I remember this so well because I was the boy – 14 years old. I came home from the neighborhood store with two big paper bags of groceries that noon and we all had enough to eat. My parents never violated their tithing again and all of us children learned the lesson from mom's prayer that morning in 1940. Tithing has been the practice of this preacher all of his life on this *Drive of Faith;* in fact, he saw to it that the college tithed on its undesignated income.

Another episode at the Academy Street residence happened that summer. My Great Uncle Art had a dairy farm in Mayville, NY. I stayed a week or two with them to help get the hay in. Neither Uncle Art nor his wife was extra clean but Aunt Grace made the best pancakes I have ever eaten. At noon, Uncle Art would go down cellar and draw off some cider from a barrel and bring it to the table. He poured me a glass and I asked him if it was hard cider, for if it was, I did not plan to drink it. I did not realize it then, but Uncle Art lied to me, assuring me that it was sweet cider. I never drank enough (only one glass) to affect me, but in later years I figured out – that was in June and apples did not come ripe until fall. He gave me cider that had been in that barrel all winter; I did not know the difference between the tastes of sweet cider and hard, so I drank it innocently.

In this *Drive of Faith* there can be times when a person might participate in something he did not realize was wrong. That principle has helped me to understand many things others could do, but I could not. This is especially true in the present generation when I behold things in our churches that would cause our Pentecostal forefathers to shake their heads with unbelief.

While working at Uncle Art's, I became acquainted with the neighbors next door by the name of Burdocks. They had several beagle hounds and wanted to give me one. I was so happy. They gave me a collar for the dog and I named it Alexander, calling it Alex for short. My brothers and sisters played with Alex and we had a great time with my pet dog when I got back home. My mother, however, did not care for my pet. She constantly complained about it and told me she wished I would get rid of it.

Finally, one Saturday I got up about daybreak, tied a rope to Alex's collar and started up the road, walking to Uncle Art's. It seems like someone came along and gave me a ride as it was several miles to Mayville. We had no money to pay for a vet to put Alex to sleep so it had to be done the old fashioned way which I will not mention here. I had left a note for mom so she knew I would be back later that day. When I arrived home and told what I had done, my siblings all felt bad. Mom could hardly believe it. Many years later she told me how bad she felt that she did not let me keep Alex. This story had a direct effect on me in this *Drive of Faith*. There have been times on the journey that I wanted something perfectly legit but found it necessary to forgo because of people I lived with – family, college campus, etc. It has not always been easy; He promised us that His way and burden was light but He did not say we would be sleeping on a bed of roses.

This helped me one time on this *Drive of Faith* when I felt I could not fulfill the vision God gave me. I had placed myself under godly men and women as my authority. My brother, Bill, was the only one who stood with me. There was no other way to have a peaceful resolution; sacrifices had to be made to keep peace. *Blessed are the peacemakers.* It was over 50 years later that I faced a situation much greater than giving up a dog. The direction those that have authority over you want to make may be different than what you feel to be right. Nevertheless, it may be necessary to bow to their wishes in order to keep from a war or serious conflict. A war like that could isolate you to a position in left field all by yourself. Perhaps this story will help some reader.

You might be asking some questions like, What happened to the vision God gave? Were you young enough when this took place to pick it up again? What happened to your authorities? I dare not answer these questions as it could hurt those that are still living. For those who want to know what I did personally, I simply went on following the will of God. I had not thought about the situation in depth until I was writing these two paragraphs, but I stood in awe when I suddenly considered what happened in the following ten years. It is only the grace of God that kept me from becoming bitter. I stand today better for the past years since I had to let the vision go. Young believer, if you are looking to travel a Drive of Faith, let me assure you there will be thunder and lightning along the way. When that happens, always remember that you have a Big Brother called Jesus and He will keep you unbelievably calm in the midst of the storm.

This last story about life on Academy Street is embarrassing to me but I promised I would tell you, so here it is. I do not know what kind of a bargain we had, but my younger brother, Buster (nick name); saved a sandwich that mom had packed for his noon lunch. He was seven years old in second grade. He shared it with me as we walked home together after school. I do not remember if I had agreed to walk home with him (almost a mile) for half his sandwich, or just what understanding we had. But I can still taste mother's delicious homemade bread, spread with peanut butter. Buster has gone to heaven now; I wonder if it will be something we will both mention when I get there? I am not sure what lesson there is in this story for the *Drive of Faith,* but perhaps you can find one for me.

From the concrete block home on Academy Street, we moved to a large house next door to Lawrence Farnham, on Webster Road in Portland, NY. Brother Farnham and his family attended the same church we did. His father, Leslie Farnham, was an elder in the church. Both my father and I worked on the grape vineyards next door; my dad trimming the vines and I pulling off the pruned vines into the middle of the row. It must have been late in the fall after the grape harvest. I attended the Brockton high school and ran track with the team. I jogged home sometimes to improve breathing and lung capacity for the races.

It was one extra cold afternoon that I froze my ears and nose while jogging. I stopped in the Post Office to get warm before continuing the trip home. There was little discomfort during the freezing, but I shall never forget the pain when ears and nose thawed out. Pacing the floor in the Post Office lobby, there was no one to tell me what to do; I just had to suffer by myself. Eventually the terrible pain eased and I continued my journey home with my jacket pulled up over my ears and around my face with space for my eyes only. I did not do much running. Most of that walk was registering in my brain the pain thawing creates when members are frozen; it made such an impression I have never frozen any part of my body since that day; I had just turned 15. I have discovered a lesson that has helped me in this *Drive of Faith* that there are times when I just had to suffer alone; not because there was no one available (the Postmaster was in the Post Office), but because I was too embarrassed to share my particular circumstance.

At that home in Portland, I remember teaching my siblings how to talk pig latin. We had a lot of fun writing and talking it when others were around. We enjoyed saying things others would have to try and figure out. In this *Drive of Faith* I have discovered there are a lot of simple fun things Christians can do without following the ways of the world.

From our home in Portland the road began an uphill climb and less than a mile was quite steep. I am not sure this happened to any of us or our neighbors at that time, but here is the story I was told about this road and high hill. In the days when cars had gas tanks close to the front dash board, it became necessary on that hill to turn the car around and back up the hill. This was especially true if one was low on gas as it was gravity fed from the tank to the cylinders; there was no fuel pump. Lesson in this *Drive of Faith;* keep your spirit full of Holy Ghost Power so you do not have to retreat when climbing a difficult hill.

Chapter 10

Kenny's Place

Our next move was to *Kenny's Place* on Prospect Road; that is how we always described it. I am not sure what the address was, but I know I attended the Mayville, NY high school during our basketball season. Not long after moving, our Aunt Connie sent a black chow dog via rail for our family to enjoy. He arrived in a crate, and being that he had traveled two days he was quite nervous. Daddy took the crate apart and let him out but the dog bit daddy's hand on the way to his freedom. It was late in the afternoon when this happened. All of us children were outside watching when daddy let the dog out. He instructed us not to touch him nor go near him.

Not long after daddy went into the house, Deacon Leslie Farnham drove in the yard and started for the porch. We children called to him warning him about our new dog that had already barked and started to follow Brother Farnham to the house. Brother Farnham, an old time Pentecostal, simply said, *"Don't worry, he can't touch me, I'm under the blood"*. He made it walking to the door without any trouble from the dog. That incident has remained in my mind for over 75 years and has inspired me many times in this *Drive of Faith*. In a day or two, the dog calmed down and became a favorite playmate for us children and a watchdog for our mom. I do not remember who named him *Teddy,* but that is what we called him all the days of his life.

It was in the summer of 1941, when we lived at Kenney's place, that I was able to get monthly jobs on farms. Dad found a farmer 15 or 20 miles away who needed a hired man and paid $25 a month with room and board. I went home on the weekends so I could attend church with the family. My job involved milking cows and helping with their care. I met a challenge while I was at this farm. A 2,200 pound Holstein bull decided he did not like me on his territory. He was usually in a pen in the barn when I went out in the fields to get the cows.

On this occasion the farmer had him in the barnyard for breeding purposes when I brought the cows in. The cows were all in the barn when suddenly that bull saw me and decided to send me to heaven. He was about 40 or 50 feet away when he bellowed and charged. Fortunately, I was near the closed 6' wooden gate. It took me only split seconds to jump, grabbing the top of the gate and catapulting over. Seconds later his front hoofs were on top of the gate which held fast and protected me. The farmer, with a pitchfork in his hand, saw this and hollered at the bull. In moments he had the bull with a pole clipped in his nose ring and led him in a docile manner to his pen. Did Satan guess in 1941 that 18 years later I would open a college on this *Drive of Faith* that would eventually challenge his kingdom with preachers around the world?

After the first month with that farmer, I was able to get a job at $30 a month, room and board, within a mile of my home. The Carlsons were kind to me as one on their own. Work began at 4 AM with a call from Mother Carlson for her son David and me to rise and go into the fields and woods for about 40 or more cows. The Carlson farm had milking machines. When milking was done, cows fed, and 7 o'clock had arrived, we were ready for breakfast. Man, what a spread. Beans, fried potatoes, eggs, bacon, milk, pie, etc. was waiting for three hungry men to devour.

I had some great experiences on that farm. One of them I will never forget. Every Wednesday night I jumped on my bike and rode 5 miles to church. Dad's job took him away working with a railroad crew during the week so my family could not get to church. I never missed all summer when I lived with the Carlsons. Travel was easy from the farm to the church; all downhill. You figured it out already; a boy pushing his bike up hill on a dirt road in the dark, arriving at the farm and quietly finding my way to my room and bed. One night the farmer thought I was already back so he locked the door and retired. Rather than knock and get him out of bed, I found a place in the hay behind the horses in the barn and slept until 4 AM.

Throughout my life on this *Drive of Faith* it has been easy to follow the pattern developed that summer on the farms. Rise early, work hard, and sleep well; it pays dividends. Did not Solomon say something about that among his famous Proverbs?

That summer Daddy bought a pair of mules, Jack and Jenny. I soon learned that mules were quite temperamental and when they made up their minds it was difficult to make a change. Daddy told us that when he was a boy he remembered a farmer who worked with mules. One day they simply would not move. The only way the farmer could win against their stubbornness was to crumble up some newspaper, lay it on the ground where the mules were standing and set it on fire. The heat of the burning caused them to move and they obeyed commands at least for that day.

However, Jack and Jenny proved themselves to Mr. Carlson on the farm. He had a large field of hay to mow and he realized his son David, and the horses with one mower were not going to get it done in time. He asked me if he thought my dad would allow me to use the mower we had and the mules to help David. Dad agreed readily and I drove the mower and mules to Mr. Carlson's farm. When I pulled up into the field, David and his father both agreed that the mules would never be able to keep up with his horses, but just do the best I could. Those mules never missed a row, around and around they went, and every time David mowed a swath, those mules mowed the same. At one point the horses disturbed a wasp nest in the hay field and David had to get his horses out of that area as fast as possible. My mules walked right through the same area, wasps landed on their back sides, they switched their tails and kept right on going as though the stinging creatures were not even there. David and his dad could not get over the endurance of those mules; they surely proved their worth. There are many lessons one can take from mules to help them in this *Drive of Faith.*

As mentioned, mules can be quite temperamental. My thirteen year old sister, Ruth, attempted to ride Jenny bareback when we lived at *Kenny's Place.* She did fine until Jenny decided Ruth should not be on her back and let her know by kicking up her heals sliding my sister off the rump landing her on the ground. I had a similar experience when trying to ride her in from the pasture. I had called and called while tramping through the brush but could not find those mules. I had just about given up when suddenly, with in ten feet of me from a covert position in the brush, one of those mules let out an audible expression I had never heard the likes of. It was nothing like a horses whinny. I could feel a shock of fear travel up and down my spine as I leaped and turned expecting to see some ferocious animal ready to attack. There was a powerful wave of sheer relief when my eyes could see these two mule heads through the leaves. Hallelujah! I am not going to be supper for an angry bear or some prehistoric animal that I had never heard or seen before. You may not understand if you have never heard a mule bray.

The mules were very docile as I encouraged them to start toward the barn. Finally I decided to ride Jenny bareback like I had done several times without incident. On her left, as is always the case when mounting an animal, I leaped into the air one moment and in less than ten seconds found myself sitting on the ground with Jenny about thirty feet in front of me kicking up her heals and headed with Jack toward the barn. Many times in this *Drive of Faith* I have encountered people much like those mules and this story has helped me treat them properly.

It was at *Kenny's Place* that I learned to drive. My dad taught me with our 1929 Model A Ford. He took me out in the field where the hay had recently been harvested and showed me how to use the clutch with my left foot and brake with my right. The first thing I noticed was that when I released the clutch the car would jerk and stall; either that or continue down the field with a jerky motion. It did not seem to run smooth like it did for my dad. At first one might be tempted to wonder if the car knew who was at the controls. With some practice, however, it seemed to purr along most of the time. I am thankful for my dad's patience as it taught me to do the same with others. I have taught many, both how to drive and in the college classroom, traveling along this road on this *Drive of Faith*.

My dad took a chance on me one evening just before dark when he sent me driving alone with my sister, Ruth. We went about ½ mile down the dirt road we lived on to get 2 quarts of milk from Farmer Farr. I was ok until the turn off the road into our drive on the way home; I was going too fast and nearly rolled the car over. It must have scared the daylights out of Ruth, although today she doesn't remember it. Again, on this *Drive of Faith,* such times have taught me to slow down on certain curves in life's road, lest I bring harm to others.

My precious sister Ruth and I attended Mayville, NY, high school when we lived at *Kenny's Place.* My parents allowed me to join the basketball team and I played on the Junior varsity as both a guard and a forward. My partner in those two positions was Ted Fisher. We were given new positions at one game while playing against Clymer, NY. It seems that three or four of the taller members on the team were caught out after midnight drinking. Coach Myers had no tolerance for anyone who broke the rules and he kicked them off the team for the rest of the season. Three things happened with that game at Clymer. The three second key-hole rule went into play. For the first and only time I played "center" during that game. Being only 5' 9", I was not the best for that position. Pictures were taken that night of high school teams throughout the nation and placed in the *Basketball Hall of Fame,* celebrating the fiftieth year of basketball. All of these things are vivid in my memory. This has taught me in this *Drive of Faith*, that even after losing (we lost to Clymer that night), one may still acquire a little fame in life if he keeps on *keeping on.*

When I first started playing on the team, I was on the bench. At one game Coach Myers was heard to say, *Put Pier in; he will get the ball.* It seemed that I had a tenacious competitive spirit that caused me to capture the basketball at any cost. I was often able to read the body language of the guards bringing the ball down the floor. As a result, many times I intercepted their passes and dribbled the ball to our basket for a layup. One thing I knew, *you cannot make points without the ball.* This kind of spirit has helped me in the *Drive of Faith* to keep my eyes on God's plan and carry it through to success.

After each game, the owner of the Mayville Ice Cream Parlor gave each player an ice cream Sundae. Forever etched in my memory is that night after a game when I was invited by a female classmate to walk her home. It would have been along a dark road and I have no idea how many miles. I found out afterwards that the girl was known among the men of my class as a real flirt and lover. It was the first time I had ever been approached with such an offer, and it certainly looked inviting. However, my daddy had instructed me not to leave the Ice Cream Parlor until Coach Myers picked me up in his car and brought me home.

My chastity was kept pure that night in spite of the pull of the flesh because God helped me to obey my dad. I knew the discipline in the woodshed that would await me when I got home. I have been forever grateful all my life for a dad who loved me enough to obey the Scriptures and not spare the rod. I realize now that daddy was young and did not always know his strength which caused some of my younger brothers to suffer unneeded scars, and for that I am so sorry. All of that taught me in this *Drive of Faith* to apply discipline carefully with love; this was especially important since I dealt with mostly teens at the college.

There are two other scenes I remember at *Kenny's Place* on Prospect Road. One was the Clark family who lived less than a mile down the road. They had a daughter who rode on our school bus and may have been in my class. She was poorly dressed and I remember feeling sorry for her condition. Her father worked his farm with a pair of yoked oxen. I remember watching him when I rode by on my $5 bicycle. It was fascinating to see someone work the land about the same as they did in the days of Jesus. I don't remember the Clark girl's name but I noticed that many of her clothes suggested they were homemade. She had poor eyesight and wore heavy glasses, all of which caused my feelings of sympathy. This memory along with scores of others along life's pathway gave me a compassion for the poor and neglected. It had a lot to do in this *Drive of Faith* with the starting of a college where I accepted any worthy student whether they had money or not.

The other scene was similar to the first. Two Polish bachelors (I'm guessing the age – somewhere in their 30s or 40s) hired me to go each morning before the bus picked us up for school. I think it was between 4 and 5 AM that I rode my bike between 1-2 miles to their farm and milked cows by hand for an hour. Those bachelors with their beards and simple methods of farming were interesting. They played a radio with music as cows are known to give more milk when there is a peaceful environment. I have wished that something could have been said to lead them to Christ, but I was not in a position to give verbal witness. All I could do at that time was *live my testimony*. The work ethics my parents had built into me, and the simple life of these bachelors, helped shape my thinking along this *Drive of Faith*. It made me an early riser, gave me a passionate, energetic desire for work, and a love for anyone regardless of their ethnic background or financial status.

Chapter 11

Winter in DeWittville

It was in the fall of 1941 that daddy said it was time to move again; we had not been able to raise the down payment for *Kenny's Place* and the 6 month's lease had run out. We moved to a farmhouse on Springbrook, Road, in DeWittville, NY. Fortunately we remained in the same Mayville school district. We acquired a small work horse by the name of *Dolly* at this new residence. Jack, the older mule, was unable to pull his share of the load so we used Dolly and Jenny as a team. It was a sad day in DeWittville when we had to give Jack to a man for – I do not know what. The man brought his rifle and daddy asked me if I would hold Jack's lead rope down at the end of our long drive while he was shot. I did not mind and I am happy now that I learned at a young age that this is just part of living. I witnessed the birth of animals and their deaths. I was 7 years of age when I watched daddy butcher our pig, smoke the bacon, and fry the pork chops.

All of this life and death had no ill effect on my life; in fact it educated me beyond my peers. My mother's mother, my nana, was horrified that my parents would allow me to see the killing and processing of an animal and I am sure she had reason for how she felt. But for me, I am so glad I was allowed to be involved in so many things that are a part of life itself. I think back to the days of Noah and his family after the flood when they started to butcher and eat meat. Those young boys all had to learn to use bow and arrow and carry bloody game out of the forest. My young education in the matters of life and death has been a blessing along this *Drive of Faith,* preparing me for unexpected bloody accidents that happen along life's pathway.

Daddy worked as the night fireman in the milk company at Mayville when we lived in DeWittville. He taught me how to take the team, an axe, a chain, and a whippletree out in the woods and cut the firewood needed in the house. I went by myself every Saturday morning, cut down a tree about 16 inches in diameter, limb it out, hook the chain around its butt and then to the whippletree, and say *giddyup* to the team. When we reached the yard next to the barn, I propped the big end of the log up on a sawhorse. My job then was to handle a crosscut saw (made for two men) and make a cut every 16 inches. Occasionally one of my brothers (Bill age 10 or Milton age 11) was instructed to help me with the other end of the saw. After the log was cut, then came the splitting. Each piece was placed on a stump where I used an axe. It took scores of swings to split the firewood into pieces small enough for the kitchen cook stove and living room heater.

Daddy helped when he came home from work and by Saturday evening the next week's supply of stove wood was safe in the woodshed. This was my job, week after week; after all, I was the oldest of the children and my parents honored me with work beyond my age. This too has helped me in life's *Drive of Faith,* and several times I found myself in a position doing things older men should be doing. Several weeks before my 19th birthday I began the task of cooking as a chef for the college of 120 (conventions – 500); I was a pastor at 19; professor in college at 28, and College president at 33. God's grace, wisdom, and strength had to be involved for this to happen.

In December of 1941, there was a humungous blizzard during the night. Daddy was the night fireman in Mayville (5 miles from our house) and usually got home quite early in the morning around daybreak. When it got to be 10 AM and daddy had not arrived in our little 1929 Model A, mother asked me to ride Jenny, the mule, down the road to see if he was stuck in the snowbank somewhere. The snow was so deep that the county snowplows could not move. A rotary machine was brought in and it had made a one lane path on the main road. I rode Jenny through snow up to her belly down our long drive to the Springbrook road which connected to the East Lake Road going to Mayville. There was no traffic as one lane had just been opened a few moments before. Jenny was moving along at a good rate when suddenly we saw daddy driving toward us. I quickly got Jenny to climb into the snowbank while daddy went by and then I followed him home. Such storms programmed me for the weather we would live in for most of our lives in the State of Maine; the place where we started the college on this *Drive of Faith.*

One day that winter I took my sister Ruth to Mayville in the Model A. I do not remember the occasion, but the event is indelibly written in my mind. As we were driving up the icy incline toward the high school, because of the icy road the car, without notice, decided to turn around and start in the opposite direction. Fortunately there was no traffic and I was able to reverse directions and complete the trip up the hill to our destination. There have been many times along life's journey when an unexpected turn of events suddenly seemed to change our direction until we realized we were going the right route in the first place. This *Drive of Faith* has had some situations like this and it was so important that we stay put in the direction God had planned.

Our home in DeWittville sat at the top of an incline with a long driveway. It was at least two hundred yards long. It was impractical to shovel the snow in the winter so daddy parked the Model A at the end of the drive just off the road. He had to drain the radiator each time it was used so it would not freeze. Our parents could not afford antifreeze or a snow blower. The old Ford had to be started by setting the spark and choke and then cranking the engine each morning.

We children had to walk the long drive and wait at the end for the school bus. My little sister, Pam, had braces on both legs to the knees and above due to the Polio she suffered as a baby. She was six years old and in first grade at that time. I carried her from the house to the road down the long drive each day. I have always considered it a great honor to have the strength and be able to bless my little sister in that way. I feel that a bond was formed at those times; Pam and I have been close in many ways along this *Drive of Faith.*

Chapter 12

A Turning Point

It was very early in the spring of 1942 – the turning point in my life when daddy decided to take a job managing a farm for a widow lady in Sugar Grove, PA. My dad asked me to go ahead of the family and do the chores on the farm until the family moved. The lady gave me a room upstairs. It was quite plain as I remember it, a bed and dresser. There was indoor plumbing for which I was thankful.

I learned to take instructions from a female while I lived and worked with this widow lady; this was a plus during the *Drive of Faith*. Many times I have found that women have valuable ideas we of the male set need. All my life, I have been a champion of the equality between men and women; the only exception being in marriage where he becomes the leader (not the boss) to set an example for his family. She fed me good until the rest of the family came.

If my recollection is right, I went to Sugar Grove the latter part of January and remained alone until the family moved sometime in March. Those weeks alone produced some maturity in my life that perhaps nothing else could have done. I was 16 at that time, and learning more everyday how to face life in this *Drive of Faith*. The farm was on both sides of Pleasant Street as one traveled east from center of town. I do not remember much about the widow lady except that she was middle age or more, normal height and slightly plump. Her meals must have been acceptable as I do not remember complaining to my parents and she must have been satisfied with my chores. She had a herd of about 20-30 cattle; I remember distinctly that there were 11 cows daddy and we boys milked by hand.

What a shock when I registered as a junior in the local high school. At Mayville high my curriculum was English, History, Typing, Latin, and probably another choice subject I do not remember. When I registered in Sugar Grove, I discovered they did not teach Typing or Latin. I was assigned to the course in Agriculture and possibly another; fortunately they did teach English and History. Seventeen years later I would need some agriculture knowledge, growing vegetables for the college I would start. It appears that God planned my life with things I did not understand at the time. Years later I came to see that my disappointment in Sugar Grove high school was a real blessing on this *Drive of Faith*. The Faith School of Theology had cattle, sheep, pigs, and many acres of gardens at different times during my tenure as president and founder for over thirty years. Those animals and gardens provided thousands of meals over that period of time and I learned some of this in Sugar Grove high school in 1942.

Daddy did not know this when he took the job of managing the farm in Sugar Grove. Friends told him about it when they knew the widow lady was giving him trouble. Her middle age husband had recently committed suicide. It all happened in this way; he went to the hardware store one morning to buy a 6 foot rope to use in leading the horses. The store manager asked him in a joking way, "W*hy don't you get 10 feet and hang yourself?"* No doubt they laughed about it, but the widow's husband said, *"Go ahead, make that 10 feet"*. When he got back to the barn he hung himself from one of the beams above the hay mow. His wife found him there after some time and called two men to take down the body. They had a knife and were about ready to cut the rope when his wife hollered, *"No, don't cut that, it's a brand new rope."*

The lady showed the same spirit when she went out one evening and removed the seat from the two horse cultivator. I had been cultivating the corn that day and she thought I ought to be walking behind the cultivator rather than riding it. After all, why make the 5 year old team of work horses pull so much. Such attitudes as this chased my dad and the family back to Westfield, NY, where he got a job in the tomato factory. Our experience on that farm helped me to realize how difficult some people can be. I met a few while directing the college on this *Drive of Faith*.

My brothers and I helped daddy milk cows by hand morning and evening while living on that farm. One large Holstein was difficult to milk; she just held on to her milk and challenged your wrist power as you struggled. I did my best to avoid sitting on that three legged stool and straining the muscles in my forearms to force moisture from some tough bovine that refused to cooperate. There was an occasion when I knew I was returning from emptying my last pail of milk in the milk house. That stingy cow was next, so I was scuffing my feet. I can still remember my dad's voice as he reprimanded me, *Pick up those feet. I want none of my boys scuffing their way through life.* That reproof challenged me many times during this *Drive of Faith*; when facing things I would like to avoid like that tough cow, I just picked up my feet and took hold of the problem. As a result of dad's discipline and example, none of his children have a lazy streak.

When the family moved to Westfield sometime in May, my parents arranged for Ruth and me to finish the school year in Sugar Grove. We stayed with friends they had made in the Wesleyan church. I stayed with Sister Carlson, a lady who had a boy with some mental disabilities. She had a couple of goats and chickens. I milked her goat for her and learned to develop a real love for goat's milk that I still enjoy. Ruth's and my stay was only a few days, maybe two weeks. I learned some things about the less fortunate people with handicaps that helped me along this *Drive of Faith.*

While in Sugar Grove I had become friends with a couple of men my age and was looking at a young brunette of the opposite sex. A week or two after returning to my parent's home, I got permission from my dad one Saturday to use the '29 Model A and drive back to Sugar Grove to see my buddies. The three of us drove to the farm where the young brunette lived. I talked to her from the window of my car. There was no particular chemistry there but it was just a nice feeling to be growing up; after all, my dad let me have the car by myself for the whole day. We stayed there less than a half an hour and started down the hilly road back to town.

At the bottom of the hill there was a small bridge with a curve on the other side. Seriously, I never was a hotrod nor did I ever try to speed with daddy's car, but trouble developed on that quick curve. The pedals (brake, clutch, and accelerator) on those Model A Fords were all metal. My foot slipped off the brake on to the gas pedal when we went over the bump on the little bridge. This caused the car to speed up around the curve and we headed for the ditch on the right side of the car. The car tipped over onto a fence and a post cracked the rear window on that side. Amazingly the motor was still going. I shut it off and the boys climbed out the window on the up-side. Someone came by and helped the boys tip the car back to an upright position. I started the engine and with a little help from the boys the old Ford was back on the road. No one was injured and we thanked God as I took the boys home and began my forty mile trip back to Westfield. Life has had some scary moments that could have been disastrous on this *Drive of Faith*. It has been only by the grace of God that this *Drive* still continues decades later. It was dusk or dark when I parked the car in the garage at 29 Clinton Street. I worked and replaced the cracked window and dad never reprimanded me.

1929 Model A Ford

Chapter 13

EBI Here I Come

It was decision time in the summer of 1942. My heart was to attend Bible college when I graduated from high school in 1943. However, because of the poor curriculum in Sugar Grove, I lacked credits and it would take me two years, graduating in 1944. My pastor was a very kind man who went to bat for me. Rev. Nelson J. Kenyon and his wife, Evelyn, have always been special in my book. His wife was my youth leader and both of these godly leaders loved the youth in their church. They arranged for me to get accepted in Eastern Bible Institute, Green Lane, PA. My first year of college was credited for my fourth year of high school.

Mr. Greene at the Florist Shoppe on Main Street (Westfield) gave me a job that summer working in his greenhouse. I labored there all summer for seventeen dollars a week. The cost to attend EBI was one hundred sixty dollars for the year. That figure included tuition, room and board. I gave my parents ten dollars a week for my room and board. It is my opinion that every able bodied person ought to pay room and board to their parents when they are working a job. One dollar and seventy cents was given in each Sunday's offering at church. My nana taught me how to go to the local Post Office and purchase savings stamps. Each week I purchased five dollars' worth and saved them toward my college payment.

I worked for Mr. Greene about ten weeks and then was able to get a seasonal job in Welch's Grape Juice factory. September/October was grape season and my pastor helped me again to arrive at the college two weeks late. This was so I could have enough money for my college bill. I was given a job at Welch's that paid next to the highest paid worker in the factory, under the foremen's salary. It paid high because of its danger; I handled five gallon glass jugs full of 180 degree grape juice. They were capable of breaking in your hands which required each worker on that job to wear long rubber aprons and rubber boots.

Work started at seven in the morning and ended at seven in the evening. The factory worked 24 hours every day during harvest season. I wanted a night job which paid a dite more, but the law would not allow me as I was only sixteen. The morning I arrived for work will never be forgotten. There were three coolers with a conveyer belt loaded with five gallon jugs of hot grape juice. Three men with rubber gloves, aprons, and boots were working tirelessly. Each man taking four jugs (one at a time) off the conveyer belt and placing them on a waist high cooler. He then pulled a rope moving his jugs through a tunnel where water sprayed to cool the juice before it got to the men on the other end of the cooler.

The seasoned men saw this one hundred fifty pound boy as I donned my apron, boots, and gloves under the direction of the foreman. One of the workers said aloud, *there were three big men on your cooler last night and they all quit; couldn't take the heat.* It was a hot atmosphere but I was hearing what I love to hear, giving me the challenge of a lifetime. I lifted every jug that bypassed the other two men and kept my cooler going all day long. The men could not believe I was still there at seven in the evening and every day after. This competitor was on the job earning every dollar he got paid. It was God who built that into my system and used this opportunity to prepare me for my life's work on this *Drive of Faith.*

A jug broke in my hands a couple of times during the four weeks I worked before leaving for college. One knob on the top of the bottle with the cork in it broke off and went flying several feet away. As that piece was in flight, it grazed my chest leaving a small wound. I did not go to the office for help; it was not really that big. It did leave a scar that has remained for seventy six years to remind me of God's grace. It was in the area of my heart and could have caused worse damage. Someone above us was looking out for this piece of clay God had chosen for the *Drive of Faith.*

It was interesting when I informed my foreman that I would not be in to work on the Lord's Day. I had, and still have, strong convictions about

Sunday being a day for rest for God's children. The foreman informed me that I would not get the bonus all workers got at the end of the season if I refused to work Sunday. My convictions cannot be bought with money, so I let him know it did not matter; I would not be there. Two weeks after I arrived at the college, an envelope came from Welch's with my bonus; Hallelujah! Some Christians tell me that every day is God's Day, but sir, that is not in the Book. The Bible declares in the very first chapter that God gave man 6 days to labor and that He wanted one day in seven for Himself alone. I taught that truth in our college and we did our best to make every Sunday a day given over to honor God. I believe with all of my heart that the success on this *Drive of Faith* has been due to a close observance of His commandments over the years.

Preparation for my college trip is rather fuzzy in my memory. Application, buying clothes and marking them all for college laundry, suitcase, pastor's counsel, are all a blur. I do remember Charles and Helen Campbell. He was my pastor's brother-in-law and they hosted a *going away party* for me a few days before I boarded a train at the local Westfield station and left for Bible College. The youth group had come together to bid me farewell. A day or two later I boarded a New York Central coach headed for Buffalo. There I transferred onto a Lehigh Valley train for Allentown, PA.

I was scheduled to arrive there in the early evening and be met by a ride to the college. However, the train wrecked alongside of the Chemung River just outside of Sayre, PA. Four or five cars tipped over on their sides after hitting a broken rail. Some feel it was an attempt by Satan to kill or cripple me, keeping me from fulfilling God's plan in this *Drive of Faith*. Buses took us to a Sayre hotel lobby where we sat for several hours waiting for transportation to Allentown. We were placed on another coach, finally arriving at our destination in the middle of the night.

I tried to sleep on one of the benches in the train station at Allentown. I had to wait for someone from the college and they could not come until morning. It was 28 miles to Eastern Bible Institute in Green Lane. I arrived on a Saturday morning. The lady driver pulled up by the men's dorm, opened the trunk to hand me my suitcase, and show me to my room. I did not notice, but found out later there were a few students looking out their windows at this new kid arriving two weeks late. I had received permission from the college to work at Welches to earn the money I needed for tuition.

A young Russell Kenneth Pier

Chapter 14

Orientation

One of those looking out the second story window was the young lady that would become my wife 10 months later. I was very young looking since I would be seventeen in just a few days. Miss Doris Rosen, looking out the window, was 21. She called to her friend, *Come here, Helene, see the cute kid who just arrived.* I did not see or hear her, and there was no chemistry working in her toward me at that time; we did not start enjoying each other until the following February.

My room was on the second floor of the new building with a pastor's son. Two other men had already tried to live with him and had asked to be moved. My roommate was a junior in the college; he had chosen to sleep on the bottom bunk. The room was quite small with 2 chairs, a small table and 2 very small chests of drawers. A small closet had a drape for a door. One of the first things my roommate showed me was a broken picture he had in his top drawer. It was of his old girlfriend; she had graduated the previous year. He got so mad at her that he took her picture and crashed it on the floor. Sometime later he told me that he and this girl had become sexually involved in the backseat of his car on campus the previous year. Of course the college officials never knew or he would have been dismissed as they were very strict on all social rules. Living with this roommate the entire year taught me many things that helped me along in this *Drive of Faith,* especially after starting our own college in Maine.

At some time in the first day or two at Eastern Bible Institute, I must have been oriented as to the rules and life on campus. The rules were very strict at this college. I really had no complaints but that does not mean the rules were never broken; I broke too many without getting caught. It all gave me knowledge and wisdom when dealing with students in this *Drive of Faith.*

I was given a duty working 14 hours each week even though I paid the full amount of tuition, room, and board; all students had to do the same. Each one of us had to keep a daily record of our time for the supervisor of duties. Seventy six years have passed at this writing, so you can understand why I do not remember the details of that orientation. These, however, are some of the expectations at the college I do recall.

Attendance at classes and chapel required ladies to wear long sleeved navy blue dresses with starched white collars and cuffs. The dress lengths were either one or two inches below the knee. A large red bow graced the collars at the front. Ladies wore hair at least to the shoulders; most of them rolled their hair on something in the shape of a crescent that hung on their shoulders. Men wore suit jacket and dress pants, shirt, and tie to all classes and chapel. Men were never allowed in shorts or bare chested on campus.

Social rules did not allow any passing of love notes or telephone calls. Use of endearing words was not allowed in public. We were not allowed to talk to the opposite sex (especially one's special friend) except for five minutes. Those five moments were before the noon meal in the foyer leading into the dining hall with all the other students present. No dating was allowed except to senior students who had been recognized by the faculty as a couple. Any violation of these social rules was met with serious discipline such as suspension or dismissal. We had assigned seats at the dining hall which were changed every two weeks; a teacher or staff member sat at the head of each table. Table manners were enforced. Waitresses brought and refilled each plate from the kitchen. Lady students (never men) served as waitresses for their 14 hour duties. Talking out of the windows of our dorms was a no-no. All lights were out at 10 PM and all students were out of bed at 6 AM during the week. We were to observe quiet hour for prayer and devotions in our rooms from 6:30-7:00 AM.

Students never felt like they were treated as children with these regulations; we were grownups that had character enough to conform to the requirements of the college. Those regulations developed lifelong habits we would need in the ministry. Jesus had a habit of rising early and going to the country side to pray; any minister is not worthy of his calling who wants to lie in bed half the morning unless his situation (health, night work, etc.) demands it. Our country was at war; we did not send children to the armed service; only men and women who could dress in uniform and follow orders. Those duties and regulations at EBI taught me many things that guided me in this *Drive of Faith* when I opened FST. The idea that youth in their late teens need freedom does not line up with Biblical teaching; the New Testament is full of regulations. *Go do your own thing* belongs in the humanistic teaching from somewhere besides the Bible.

My first duty was scrubbing the hall floor and stairs in the ladies dorm on my hands and knees. They were the old wooden floors in the old part of the building. As a young single man I did not mind that duty. I got a chance to meet all the young ladies at the Institute as they had to pass through the old dorm to get to the new. I remember two incidents that were interesting. One was the Saturday morning when I was about three steps down scrubbing away. Just then Miss Mary Garns, a prim and proper senior in her middle or late twenties, started down the stairs on my right. For some reason she lost her balance and was falling head first down the stairs. She would have been seriously injured or even broke her neck, but I reached out quickly with my right arm and grabbed her across the waist. Embarrassed, and with a red face, she properly thanked me.

The second incident was later on in the year when I was considering Doris Rosen for a special friend. She stopped to talk with me (which was a no-no) on her way through to her room in the new dorm. The place was the little hall at the bottom of the stairs which led out into the long hall to the outside exit. We had not been talking long when we heard the footsteps of the matron approaching down the long hall. Doris quickly slipped behind the drape on the hall closet until Miss Helen Rosenbaum had gone by. The matron was known to turn people in for breaking rules, so we were glad she disappeared without knowing. By the way, Miss Rosenbaum married and became a real friend to both of us on Cape Cod, MA. I had the opportunity to minister in the church she attended dozens of times.

A young Doris Rosen

Chapter 15

Exciting Moments at EBI

The shenanigans of my roommate during the year I spent at Eastern Bible Institute are unbelievable. Some of his mischief was done alone, such as in the night after hours when he went down and opened the back window to the kitchen and stole an orange or two. Another was a time he tried to get me to accompany him as he got into his Pontiac Coup that sat on a slope not far from the dorm. This was after hours, of course. He coasted with lights out into the lower drive without starting the car until he passed President Swift's house. It was a long drive to the roadway and then on down to the small village of Green Lane. He spent an hour or more in the village but he did not share with me what he did. Arriving back to campus he drove in the upper drive, turned his lights out, and eventually shut his motor off, coasting back to his original beginning. He did not get caught on either of these occasions.

There were two other incidents that were more serious. One afternoon he came in the room with an empty two-gallon oil can and a long clothes line rope. He tucked them away in the closet and let me know I would see later what he was doing. That evening, somewhere around eleven or twelve o'clock, Dave and Glenn from next door came in our room. The three opened our window, took the empty oil can with the rope tied to the handle, and threw it down.

It landed on the wooden steps that led to the offices on the floor below us. They pulled on the rope so that the can went bangity, bang, bang, down the steps, making an awesome noise in the dead of the night. With great speed they pulled the can up and in the window. Tucking it away with the rope in the closet, they carefully watched out the window for any reaction.

Sister Swift, the President's wife, was in her office. She came quickly to the door, stepping out on the landing where the can first fell, and looked all around on the ground below. She never once looked upward and considered it coming from a window. In a few moments she returned to her office. This happened in the winter of 1942-43 at the height of World War Two. No doubt the incident might have blown over and been forgotten except for one of the lady students. Peggy Varghese thought the Germans were bombing and brought the whole girl's dorm to the halls. She had a serious trauma spell and only after an hour or more of prayer and comfort was there any peace in the dorm. No official ever found out who was the master mind behind the cause of turmoil that night.

Dave, Glenn, Bill, and my roommate almost got into serious trouble one afternoon when they got intoxicated. They bought a gallon of unprocessed apple cider and some raisons about a week previous to their escapade. Each one had a small glass of the fresh cider to drink, after which they dumped in a few raisons and placed the gallon glass jug next to the radiator. After a week or ten days when the boys were sure fermentation had taken place, they got together in the room next to mine and drank the contents.

It affected the boys in different ways. Bill went down stairs to his room and regurgitated, while Glenn and Dave spent the evening in their room laughing and carrying on as intoxicated. With my roommate it was an entirely different story. Sweating profusely, he accompanied his girlfriend and two other ladies as part of a quartet. They traveled with President Swift to a church that evening for ministry. My roommate made sure the President and the ladies were ahead of him as he walked down the aisle so he could take hold of each pew as he felt wobbly. Fortunate for my roommate, he was able to fake himself through the singing and return with the group to campus without anyone noticing. Rev. Walter Beuttler, the dean of men, must have heard something about the cider as he called all of us boys together and forbid anyone to bring cider of any kind on campus.

It might have been because I was the youngest in the crowd, but when I refused to be involved in any of these tomfooleries, the older male students went ahead without me. As you will see in future segments, I did not have a spotless record when it came to social rules; but I was blameless in these shenanigans. All of this helped me in the *Drive of Faith* when I started the Bible college. My advice to anyone attending Bible college was, *choose your friends wisely.*

Life for me was different at Eastern Bible Institute; parental authority, which I had always respected, had been replaced with the regulations of the college and the Dean of Men. One of the regulations stated that all students had to be in their room (the purpose was to study) when they were not in class during certain hours of the day. John Bergstrom, from across the hall, was visiting my roommate in the early afternoon when they heard the Dean's footsteps in the hall. John quickly ducked in the closet and waited while Bro. Beuttler (dean) visited with my roommate. It was a warm spring day, making it extra warm in the closet. That prankster of a roommate kept asking questions of the Dean to prolong his stay and make it more miserable for Johnny. Finally the Dean left and Johnny emerged from the closet soaking wet with sweat and quite upset with my roommate.

Another time something similar happened to me when I was visiting across the hall during study time. Here comes Dean Beuttler down the hall and into the closet I went. My stay was not long and I would have got off scot free except Someone above had seen me. The Holy Spirit would not let me get by with that. He sent jolts of conviction until the only way to get relief was to knock on the Dean's door and confess what I had done. Both of these closet events helped me in this *Drive of Faith* when I had to deal with college students. It taught me mercy for those who repented and an inquisitive eye when dealing with others.

Bedbugs! What a horrible thought, but that is what happened in one room across the hall. Snow was on the ground as I watched the men throw out the mattress with bugs. I do not remember just what method they used to rid the room of those evil pests, but eventually over a period of days it became clean. In the meantime, I did what I had been taught by our old-fashioned holiness pastor; I stood in the hall when I was alone, and pronounced the covering of the blood of Jesus on the lintel and door jambs of my room, asking God to protect this abode from any bedbugs or pestilence of any kind. I can truthfully say that my roommate and I enjoyed a room free from such evils. Some of the other rooms got infected, but never where I lived. This too helped me in this *Drive of Faith;* I have had several chances to use His blood covering for protection since that time. Once was when the college moved to Charleston and took over a dorm building where drugs had been secretly used. We walked through the dorm, Bibles in front of us, pleading the blood of Christ for His cleansing.

Four little incidents will take your reading time before I start the love affair that ended in a nearly 60 year marriage. The first one I am embarrassed to write about, but it has a bearing on my *Drive of Faith;* it happened during English class in my first year of college. There I was, a young, just turned 17 year old kid, sitting behind a row of girls. Red haired Margery Barnes sat directly in front of me. Her sweater was draped over her shoulders and the sleeves hung down the outside of her chair. What made me do it, I don't know, but it was probably that boyish desire I have to tease females. I tied the two arms of her sweater together around the top of her chair so the chair would cling to her when she stood up. Somehow, Brother Buchwalter, our English teacher, saw that I was up to something and it resulted in me being asked to leave the room.

Nothing more was said, but the next day was Saturday when the men that wanted to could gather in the men's lounge and pray. I tried praying but it wasn't working; the heavens were brass. When I enquired of the Lord, He reminded me of the sweater and English class. I knew what that meant, so I left the lounge and made my way to Bro. Buchwalter's cabin. Timidly, I knocked on the door. In just a few seconds that seemed to me like an eternity, there was a man standing where the door was. Stammering to the best of my ability, I let him know how sorry I was for my behavior in his class, asked his forgiveness. I assured him it would not happen again. He patted me on the shoulder and told me I was forgiven; we said our *good byes* and I walked on air back to the lounge where my prayers had static free wires straight to the throne. This incident taught me in this *Drive of Faith* that there are times when some students need that kind of embarrassing discipline.

The second incident is much the opposite; it happened in Bro. Arnold's Ancient History class. The students had all chosen their seats in the chapel for the exam that day. I sat on the end next to the aisle and four male students sat next to me in my row. I was not entirely aware of what they were doing, but towards the end of the exam I surmised some had been cheating. A day or two passed when Bro. Arnold sent for all five of us boys. We were asked to meet in his office. He had five tests laid out in order and asked us to pass by and notice the similarity in the answers. He did not need to make any accusations; it was all plain. Each man bowed his head and said the word guilty as they passed by until it came my turn. How glad I was to be able to say, *not guilty*. The student next to me had copied my answers and each of the others had done the same down the row. This incident helped me realize that even in Bible college some students will continue their high school sins and will need discipline, love, and prayer to overcome. Another good blessing added to the *Drive of Faith*.

Chapter 16

A Love Affair Begins

It was Thanksgiving time at EBI and everyone was leaving campus. I had no way home but Bro. and Sis. Wise offered me a ride to NY Rt. 17 at Painted Post. They were going home to Bath, NY, and were giving Rev. Allan Swift, the school president a ride as he was preaching that weekend in their area. They left me off in late afternoon and I started hitchhiking west on Rt. 17 toward my home in Westfield. I walked several miles without a ride until it was extremely dark. My eyes were drooping with need for sleep and I saw a large hay stack in the field. I maneuvered over the pasture fence and made it to the stack only to find it was a huge manure pile. That ended my desire to sleep for the time being; now back to the road and hiking.

Few vehicles were on that road at 2, 3, and 4 o'clock in the morning. To make a long story shorter, I got enough rides to get me to Clinton Street in Westfield, NY, by 10 AM Thanksgiving morning. Our family Thanksgiving dinner in 1942 consisted of macaroni and meatless tomato sauce; we may have had some homemade bread and pie, but I really don't remember. On that Sunday following Thanksgiving, I had to be at the church in Bath, NY for the Sunday night meeting so I could ride back to EBI. The college class schedule was very tight; classes on the Wednesday before Thanksgiving and on Monday morning after that holiday. My Thanksgiving vacation at EBI helped me when I set the calendar at FST so many years later. We reached out to those who did not have. It also helped me to persevere on this *Drive of Faith* when things look dark and impossible.

It is hard to remember the details of 74 years ago but I managed to get home for Christmas vacation in 1942. It was in time to help the family move from Westfield to Pecore St. in Portland, NY; approximately 8-10 miles. My job was to drive our family car (1929 Ford), loaded with clothes and furniture. Daddy had built an extension over the rear bumpers of our Ford and loaded a dresser and boxes on that platform. With the back seat full of clothes and whatnot, and my sister, Ruth, in the front seat, I started east on Rt. 20 to Portland. Several inches of snow had covered the ground and though the road had been plowed the going was icy and great care was necessary in driving.

About half way to Portland, a fast moving car came up behind me while there was traffic going west coming toward me. The man behind me tried to brake on the icy road and slid off to the right, breaking a mail box and perhaps damaging the front of his vehicle. The posted speed limit was 40 MPH on that highway, but on that icy road and loaded so heavy, I was creeping along between 20-25 MPH. The man who slid off the road was irate and pulled up beside me and flagged me down. Remember, I am only 17, just had my license a short time, and I am standing face to face with a grizzly looking man twice my size in his 50s. He pulls out some kind of badge and informs me that the posted speed is 40 MPH on that road and I was supposed to be going that fast. I told him that I was sorry and would try to do better. We both got back in our cars and he took off.

I chuckle when I think of it now and of all the lessons I can get from that in this *Drive of Faith*. I will leave you with just one at the present; sometimes older individuals with fake credentials may try to lead young people down the road of worldly ideas. I am acquainted with some in the past who did their best to pull students and graduates away from Dr. Pier's strict conformity to God's Word. Some succeeded only to see worldliness destroy lives.

The family had moved and was well situated on Pecore Street when it was time for me to return to college. Little did I know that seven months later I would spend my wedding night in that home. How I made the trip back to Green Lane is lost to my memory; I have no idea. Back at EBI I am now ready to complete the first semester and begin another step in my education for the *Drive of Faith*. In the next four months things would happen that would have life changing effects on this boy's future.

Remember the Saturday morning I arrived on campus last fall? The girl I married was looking out the window and noticed this new student getting out of a staff members car. She called to her friend, Helene Dunitz, and said, *Helene, come see the cute kid who just arrived.* Later on that fall semester I started to notice a classmate named Bette Davis. Evidently I must have given Bette some reason to believe I was interested in her. She went to the girl I eventually married and asked for prayer and advice. Bette got some negative advice and the program stopped.

Another interesting event happened at dinner time in the dining room. My assigned seat that week was at the President's wife's table and the server was none other than the girl I married 9 months later. The menu was pea soup, my favorite, and I ate plenty. After all, at 17 I was a growing boy. It was the server's job to take each person's bowl back to the kitchen and have it filled. As I remember, that particular day, I ate 7 small bowls. The server sat the seventh bowl down in front of me and said emphatically; *There, brother, I would rather pay your board than feed you.* Everyone at the table let out a little laugh, including me. Sister Swift (the President's wife) said in a joking manner, *Russell, I think next year we will need to charge you more for your room and board.* That brought on some more quiet laughter. I use the word quiet for in those days it was not polite to make loud noises at the dinner table. All of this helped me understand at least three things on this *Drive of Faith;* 1) that young men need plenty to fill their plates, 2) that cute kids have to be careful about who is watching them, 3) etiquette (speaking softly) at the table or anywhere in college is important.

When I returned from Christmas vacation, I felt convicted about looking at any girl when I had a female friend back in my home church. That girl came from a fine Christian family and we had been talking together almost 2 years. We had never kissed or hugged and I think I might have held her hand once or twice. She told someone that I was slow (she meant in showing affection). I was extremely bashful around girls. When the young people of our church played *Post Office* and the situation demanded that I go into the back entry with one of the girls to kiss, I would say, *let's go back in and just pretend we kissed?* They always agreed and I escaped those many thrills that could have been mine.

Now, I'm in college, and it is time to be more serious. So I write the girl back home and break off our relationship. I did not know this until years later, but she must have had a real love for me. She went to Pastor Kenyon's wife sobbing and Sister Kenyon had to take time to calm her, pray, and encourage her. This has helped me many times through the years in this *Drive of Faith.* I sat with many broken hearts when student lovers broke up. *Faith* is important when things go wrong and is definitely an ingredient for broken hearts.

In January of 1943, the college started giving an opportunity for social fellowship between the sexes by offering an hour on Sunday afternoons for couples to meet in the lady's lounge. We were not allowed to hold hands or use any other PDA (public display of affection), but we could sit together and talk. I had recently noticed this Doris Rosen and knew she did not have a male friend. I am a lonely 17 year old that had a craving for close friendship built into me. It took a lot of courage, but I asked her if she would like to sit and talk some Sunday afternoon when the others gathered in the lady's lounge. She answered, *If I get my homework done.*

On one Saturday evening late in the month of January, I inadvertently happened to be in the men's room looking out the window at the star lit sky. This happenstance was not planned in anyway. At the same time I noticed a head move out of the lady's room window about 30 feet to my left. The girl had not seen me, but when I discovered who it was, I gave a slight cough to get her attention. She was as surprised as I was to see me. We talked briefly and softly for a very few moments as this was against regulations. I asked again if she would meet me in the lady's lounge the next day, and she agreed to be there as she had finished her homework. We left quickly as we did not want to be caught talking out the window.

Without any effort from either of us, on that January Sunday afternoon, a bond was formed between Russell Kenneth Pier, Jr. and Doris Estelle Rosen. How she knew I had a girl back home, I don't remember, but the first words that came from her mouth that Sunday afternoon were, *I want you to know, Bud, that I don't play second fiddle to anyone.* I was quick to inform her that I had already written and broke off relationship with Florence. And that the letter I sent had nothing to do with any feelings I might have for her or anyone else. I wrote the letter because I felt moved of God to do so. With that out of the way, we got down to business and started talking about our families, our childhood, and our commitment to God. All those social rules at Eastern Bible Institute helped me with discipline in my own life and the development of the college I started on this *Drive of Faith.*

Chapter 17

A Chapter You Will Never Believe

It was one Saturday evening when all was quiet in our dorms at Eastern Bible Institute. On the second floor of the new building there was a short hall between the lady's and men's dorm that housed a variety store on one side and a small library (about 12x12) on the other side. Locked doors at both ends of the short hall separated the two dorms. The store was open and library available for about one hour each afternoon. Staff members were always present during the store hour and all social rules were in force. But that Saturday evening, after store hours, Doris obtained a skeleton key, unlocked the door to that short hall, stepped inside, and locked it back up again. She then proceeded across the hall to the door leading to the men's dorm and gave a quiet cough. I knew exactly what time she would be there, so I quietly coughed back (after making sure there were no men in my hall to see this). She unlocked the men's door, let me in, and locked it back up; there we were alone for the first time to enjoy a few moments together in the dark.

We stepped into the small library and took seats at a table. We talked for some time when I reached over and stroked the back of her hand and wrist. I had never done this to any girl before, but she said to herself, *"This fella has been around"*. We could hear Bob Kremples, the monitor and his roommate talking in their men's dorm room that butted the library. One of us inadvertently moved a chair that made a noise. We heard Bob say to his roommate, *"Sounds like someone is in the library. I better check it out"*.

I moved quietly and quickly to the window (2 ½ stories up) and hung outside on the brick sill with my fingers, while Doris closed the window and sat back down. Fortunately for us, Bob did not have a key, so all he did was try the door knob and went back to his room. Doris opened the window and I pulled myself up by my fingers and crawled back into the room. We decided it was time to leave, kissed for the first time, and I quietly slipped out into the empty men's hall and into my room without being seen. Doris locked the door behind me and went back to her room without being noticed. Unless the authorities of Eastern Bible Institute are reading this story, none ever knew this happened; actually I'm sure they are all waiting for their resurrection just now.

The next day I wrote Doris a short note telling her what a thrill I got from her kiss in the library; after all, it was the first time in my life I had ever kissed a girl on the lips. When she read that, she shook her head in disbelief. You see, having never necked, hugged, or kissed, I simply flattened my lips out tight and Doris thought she was kissing a telephone pole; she got no pleasure of any kind and thought sure she had picked the wrong man. She was 4 years older than I and had boyfriends before, so she knew how to kiss. She had never been immoral, but at 21 it is not strange that she had gone out with young men. I think it is time to stop writing about kissing; I will just add that it did not take me long to learn from such a wonderful lover as Doris Rosen.

You can bet that the library was not the end of our breaking rules. Doris often retired after hours to the girls sewing room on the first floor to talk with God and worship alone. It was there that the Holy Spirit told her to get a paper and pencil. She did so and took dictation from the Lord concerning our friendship. It was a beautiful message placing God's approval on our future union; this became a great bulwark defending our marriage throughout the years. I suggest that every couple, before you go very far in your friendship get a *Word from God* that will help safeguard your future together. I have forgotten many of the words in that message, but I had the last sentence placed on our tombstone; *Together you shall lay sheaves at the Master's feet.*

Sometime after that message came, Doris made me aware that there was a sewing room window right off the outside steps that was easy to open and enter. During the day I walked by the location and checked it out. On a designated night, after lights out (10:00), I was able to quietly slip out of the dorm and make my way around back where the stairs and window were located. Doris had the window open a couple of inches so I could quietly shove it up and enter the small sewing room. Wow, here we were, the first time together since the library, and no one to bother us.

We sat on the floor side by side with our backs to the wall. We did not want to be caught and dismissed from college, so we limited the time to less than an hour; I assure you it was the greatest, most exciting hour of my life thus far. There was no touching except to hug and kiss, but that was enough for a 17 year old. Remember, he had never been alone with any girl and now he sat beside someone who thought he was the best she had ever known. I quietly slipped out the window and walked on air back to my dorm room, climbed into bed, and dreamed away the night. That was the only time we met in the sewing room. This incident reminded me years later, in this *Drive of Faith,* that young people will find a way to be together, if only for a few minutes, whenever they can.

That year we shared valentines with each other. I do not remember any words on the one I gave her, but she sent me one with two bicycle wheels; each wheel was saying to the other, *Let's go around together!*

Sometime in late March or early April, Doris got word that her parents were coming from New Jersey to see her. They made arrangements with the college dean to take Doris and me to dinner at a restaurant in Pennsburg, a town nearby. I was as nervous as a cat on a hot tin roof. I was meeting my girlfriend's parents and eating with them; this was out of my comfort zone. I had seldom been in a restaurant. I sat with Doris, facing her parents next to a window looking out on the diner's parking lot. Her mother was a godly woman of about 43, and easy to talk to. Her father was a full blooded Jew and unsaved. His parents died when he was a young child, and being the youngest son in the family, his brothers robbed him of his share of the parent's estate that was left to all their children. As a result, Mr. Rosen carried some baggage through life, forsook his religion, and married Doris' mother, a Gentile.

So here we are, in a diner ordering a meal for which I was told I did not have to pay. I do not remember what I ordered, but I'm sure I ordered one of the less expensive meals as I wanted to make a good impression on these new people I was meeting for the first time. I was glad my parents along with my maternal nana had taught me table manners. The meal, our conversation, and trip to Pennsburg and back were uneventful. I do not remember what was said about me after they left, but when school closed in May, her parents invited me to go to their home to visit for a few days. This whole experience helped me in *The Drive of Faith* to realize how important it was to know manners of all kinds. As a result, when I made up the curriculum for the college we started, I made sure there was room for a course on etiquette. It was taught for several years in our college and many students have thanked us for the instructions we gave in that course.

My roommate often made cute remarks about my relationship with Doris Rosen. For instance, when Doris and I wanted to communicate we would often go to our open windows and give a little cough; this would bring the other one to the window. My roommate would say, *got consumption, go see D R* (Doris Rosen). Or when Doris would write me a note, she would indicate this with the cough out the window and then go to that door by the library I wrote about. Without opening the door to the men's dorm, she would give a little cough, I would cough back, and she would slip the note under the door for me. One day I brought the note in, took it out and laid the envelope on the table. On the back of the envelope it had a printed message reading, *Jesus Never Fails.* My roommate saw it and said to me, *Jesus never fails, slip it under the door.* From this experience I learned in this *Drive of Faith* it was practically useless to ban young people from communicating with one another; love finds a way to express itself. It was better to concentrate on less physical contact and let other communications take their course.

Another means of communication for Doris and me was through the Morris Code. I had learned the same through Boy Scouts and taught her the basics. On Saturdays the ladies would do their personal laundry and climb up into the attic which was over both the men and women's dorm but only accessible through the lady's area. Doris would take her laundry up to the attic and then find a spot directly above my room and tap out a message in the Morris Code. I cannot remember if I was able to communicate through the ceiling or not, but at least I heard that she loved me, etc.

One other way we communicated was through the deaf language. My deaf brother had taught me the deaf alphabet years before, and I passed it on to Doris. We used it when we were sure no one was watching, in the dining hall, chapel, out the dorm windows, etc. It was most convenient that I had somehow (smile) learned both the Morris Code and Sign Language as a young boy. It simply shows one in this *Drive of Faith* that childhood events and learning can go a long ways in helping to communicate later on in life.

In the spring of 1943 the college had a short vacation around Easter time. It was impossible for me to travel home, so I made arrangements to remain on campus. I am not sure why Doris did the same; she only lived a little over one or two hours traveling time from Green Lane and I am sure her parents would have come for her had she asked. Perhaps there was an attraction at the college; at any rate, she decided to stay. I do not remember what we did with our days; perhaps we worked on the campus to earn our keep. I do remember, however, one glorious night when I found myself quietly easing my way up the stairs of the lady's dorm to her room. I have forgotten her room number but I do recall who was waiting on the other side of the door. There was no settee that we could sit on together, so we had no choice but to place ourselves, sitting next to each other on her bunk bed.

Conveniently, I have forgotten all that happened during that brief hour, but I do know there was no improper touching or immorality. And yet, it was one glorious experience I shall never lose from my memory. We knew that night we were meant for each other and we pledged to keep ourselves pure until our wedding night. I was able to slip quietly out of the dorm without being detected; our meeting was so successful that we agreed not to attempt such a tryst again. I hope no one reading this is in an official position at Valley Forge University (EBI's present name). Please don't mar our spotless record or deduct any points from our grades. In this *Drive of Faith* I discovered dozens of couples over the fifty years I spent with the college who disobeyed social rules while attending FST. I never allowed their grades or deportment to be changed. Only two people's status was changed after their graduation; one because she lied to me about her marriage situation and the other because he never returned to complete a failed course for which he had promised. Neither of these concerned social rules.

Chapter 18

Events Affecting My Future in May and June

On May 10, 1943, Eastern Bible Institute celebrated its third graduation. All the students were sent home for the summer. My sweetheart's parents invited me to spend a few days at their home in New Jersey before making the trip of several hundred miles back to Portland, NY. I do not remember how much of a struggle I had with that decision but I finally decided to accept their generosity. Doris' father was a gold seal engineer at Otis Elevator Company in Newark, NJ, and her mother cooked lunches for students in the local school. They lived in a large house in the beautiful upper-class town of Mountain Lakes, NJ. They were from middle class America while my family was much less affluent.

During the two or three weeks that I stayed at the Rosen's, Doris' Aunt Mildred had to be confined to a bed because of severe back pain. In those days it was common for the church people to gather at the sick person's home and spend some time in prayer, anoint with oil, and watch God heal. Sister Rosen, Doris, and I went to Aunt Mildred's one evening to join with about 20 other church people and pray. Pastor Caughey was not able to be there, so when it came time to anoint and pray for Aunt Mildred, they handed the oil to me. I was dumbfounded; a first year college student, never had anointed anyone in my life, and they wanted me to anoint and pray? You got to be kidding. But the more I refused, the more the people were determined I should do it. Forced into the situation, I took the oil while everyone was closing their eyes and praying, and poured about an eighth of a cup on her head; I did not know how it was done. I said a simple prayer and heard Aunt Mildred come up in bed, shouting praises, as she exclaimed, "*Something came from my toes up through my legs and back, and the pain is absolutely gone."*

That incident did a great deal to help me in this *Drive of Faith*. It was through this healing incident that Holy Spirit made real to me that He had endowed me with some of the Gifts of Healing. Over the many decades of ministry there have been many touched by God; to Him be all the glory forever and ever.

One incident, on the side line, that happened while at Aunt Mildred's home is worthy of mention. Berdie Fedor was a classmate of mine in Eastern Bible College and came from the same church as Doris. He wanted his teenage sister to meet me. He brought her over to me as the people were milling around and talking. When she shook my hand, she was reluctant to let go, and for much longer than necessary, she hung onto my hand although I tugged gently to take it away. I did not want to cause a scene, but finally she let go. Doris was not at my side when that happened, but she had seen the incident without knowing how much I tried to loose myself. Nothing was said until we got in the backseat of her mother's car. Doris seemed cold and distant, and I had no idea what was going on in her mind. It took sometime before I got her to tell me. Immediately I began the repair work by explaining in detail what had happened. Finally she was warm again and life proceeded, but it left an indelible impression on me for this *Drive of Faith;* keep your wife (female friend, in this case) nearby when greeting anyone who might have designs that were not wholesome.

In two or three days I received word that my parents needed me at home. It was one dark evening that Mother Rosen took me to the Greyhound bus station in Denville, NJ. My trip took me to Buffalo, where I changed busses for Portland, NY, the home of my family. I will never forget the kindness of Mr. and Mrs. Rosen; they would have kept me all summer if I could have stayed.

A job was waiting for me when I returned and I started work immediately on a construction crew for the Nickle Plate Railroad. One of my early Sunday school teachers at the Westfield Assembly of God was my foreman. He trained me to use an eighty pound jack hammer to break up old stone construction under bridges the crew was repairing. This back breaking, muscle building job taught me in this *Drive of Faith,* God's provision may come from heavy work but He gives the strength and stamina to survive it.

During the week, the crew slept in a railroad car fitted with bunks and ate in another car fitted with kitchen and dining facilities. That summer we worked on a bridge crossing a large creek in the community of Silver Creek, NY. It was 35 miles from the Westfield Assembly of God, but each Wednesday night I hitch hiked to prayer and Bible study. I had no other way to travel. One night on my way back to Silver Creek I got a ride with a man who had been drinking liquor. I caught up on my prayer life as he wove back and forth at 80 miles per hour. Speed limits in those days were about 45MPH. I discovered on this *Drive of Faith* one never knows what provision will be afforded but in spite of drunken drivers or otherwise, God gets you there safely.

Shortly after I returned home in the summer of 1943, my youth leader asked me to speak at a Friday night youth service. The youth leader was Rev. Eleanor Kenyon, wife of my pastor. She would not take no for an answer. She gave me ample notice, probably a week or two. I had learned a lot at Eastern Bible Institute and wanted to use some of that new knowledge for my message. I wish I could remember what went through my mind at that time, but time and the trauma of that experience have caused me to forget. I must have had some thoughts about displaying some of the knowledge I had gained, because I chose to speak on the Gifts of the Holy Spirit in 1 Cor. 12. That should be a profound message for someone who had been preaching for some time, but I must have thought I could handle this new found truth. I remember studying hard and praying a lot before I finally put together an outline for what I thought would be about a half hour message.

The youth services were held in a small chapel on the west side of the auditorium. As I remember it, there were probably between 25 and 40 present. After the preliminaries I was introduced but I have no recollection of the moment; I was too nervous – something like a cat on a hot tin roof. The next ten minutes are forever engraved on my memory. Stammering and stuttering, I spit out the message in the best way I could. I am sure when I finished everyone in that audience wondered why I should think of preaching. Charles Campbell, the youth leader's brother, reached out his hand when I left the platform and walked down the aisle. As he shook hands he said, "Good try, Russell, better luck next time." I am sure that made me feel like I was to be a second Billy Sunday and would end up taking my generation by storm (a hyperbole).

Poppa and Nanna Rosen

Chapter 19

Rosen and Pier Become One

Three days later was a resurrection day. Saturday afternoon at about two o'clock I was sitting at the dining room table with tablet and pen. I had just returned home from the construction crew on the Nickle Plate Railroad and was prepared to write my darling Doris. In fact, I had written the first sentence; *My Darling little girl, I wish you were here right now.* My siblings were playing outdoors and my mother was sitting in the living room enjoying the cool breeze coming through the open screened door off the porch.

At that moment my sister Pam came to the door and said, *"Russell, there's a girl out here that wants to see you".* I was surprised and replied, *"I'm busy; I'm not interested in seeing any girl."* Thinking back, I probably thought Pam was joking. Just then one of my siblings said, *"What if it is Dorie?"* (that was what they called her). I jumped up from the table and rushed out to see; just as I thought, there was no girl. But my siblings were acting strange around a large flowering bush in the front yard, so I proceeded to look around the bush and who do you suppose was scooched down hiding there but Doris E. Rosen. I need not tell you what the next sixty seconds was like. After the final greeting of the lips, we came inside and listened as she told the story.

When Doris returned home at the request of her parents, she could not eat and her mother found her lying across her bed weeping. She told the story of her stay at our home, purchase of wedding rings, etc. She was weeping as she talked telling her mother how much she loved me. Her mother said, *"I had no idea you loved him that much. You are twenty two years old and of course you can marry him if you feel this way".* Sister Rosen may have been thinking of her own marriage that she would celebrate in six more days; a marriage where she and her husband had eloped because they loved each other so much.

At any rate, she went to work and got Doris ready for marriage and the trip back to Portland, NY. A wedding dress was borrowed from Doris' sister, Pearl. Sister Rosen got material and made a veil, and purchased white shoes. Before you know it, on Friday evening Doris was on a Greyhound traveling from one end of New York State to the other, landing in Portland just after the noon day hour. When she changed buses in Buffalo, she sent a telegram to me – a telegram I still have not received. Our family was too poor to have a telephone at that time. When she got off the bus where Pecore Street meets the Main Road (Route 20) in Portland, and I was not there to meet her, she had all kinds of thoughts going through her girlish mind. She went to a ladies door and asked if she could leave her suitcases on her porch until she came back from our house. Doris proceeded to walk down Pecore (about one quarter of a mile) and hide behind a bush where my siblings were playing. She told them not to say who was there.

After retrieving her suitcases from the lady's porch, we began to plan for a wedding the next day. It was a busy Saturday afternoon as we made trips to the town clerk to get the marriage license. My mother had to sign for me because I was not yet 18. From there we went to the florist in Westfield for a gardenia to place on the top of the white Bible Doris would carry down the aisle. We got a roll of paper for a runner on the aisle and contacted the best man and the maid of honor. That evening we practiced the ceremony and program with Pastor Kenyon.

Doris and I attended Sunday school and worship service at my home church on the corner of Clinton and Franklin Street in Westfield. I do not remember what Pastor Kenyon said in the morning service, but I am sure he invited everyone to the 7PM wedding that evening. The wedding party consisted of Ted Belardi as the best man, Carolyn Marino as the maid of honor, Ruth Helen Pier as a bride's maid, and Pamela Pier as the flower girl.

After the 7 PM ceremony, we went to my nana's house on Main Street in Westfield, until the service at church was over. My folks picked us up and we went home with them to Pecore Street in Portland, about six miles. A few of the church people came and we enjoyed cake and fruit punch. We stood up, walking around as the table was not large enough for all of us to sit. Doris and I slept in the northwest bedroom, to the right at the top of the stairs just past the bathroom.

How late we slept, I do not remember, but we took a mile walk to Lake Erie when we woke up in the morning. We had often walked that mile during the past few weeks to stand on the shore and dream as we stared at the steam of light left on the water by the setting sun. That stream of light had heard us as we talked about the ups and downs of life, the hidden rocks, and the distance from where we stood to the gates of that City. When we stood there the day after our wedding, we became aware that the journey had begun. The mid-day sun left no light path, but we imagined those we had seen day after day at supper time. When I look back at it now, I confess to you that the long journey has been a *Drive of Faith,* a trip I look forward to finishing triumphantly by His grace.

On our walk back to the house that Monday noon, we crossed the rails of the Nickle Plate Line for which I worked. Wouldn't you know, at that very hour my crew was moving from Silver Creek, NY, to Peach Street in Erie, PA? Our men had just finished construction of the bridge piers in Silver Creek and the diner and sleeper cars, plus all the construction equipment were on their way at noon time to the new site. We waved back when the crew waved at us from the slow moving work train.

Sometime that afternoon we made a trip to Westfield where we rented an apartment on South Portage Street within two blocks of the center of town. The first week at our new apartment we did not have much money or food. Doris did the best she could but I ate with the crew in Erie; it was difficult for me to think of my wife with so little. I do not remember how many nights I was able to get home that week or any week as I had no transportation for the 35 mile trip. I rode with some of the men when we finished work on Friday nights. The men picked me up at my apartment on their way to the job on Monday mornings.

I do remember one evening being home and someone had given us a ripe cantaloupe. We cut it in half and I fed her half to her while she was mending some of my clothes. After I had finished feeding her the half designated as hers, I picked up my half and started feeding her more. When she had eaten quite a bit of it (without knowing she was eating my half), I said to her, *"this is good, have you had enough?"* She thought I was kidding with her and just wanted to finish her half, so she just kept on eating while I fed her mine. Finally, she said, *"ooh, I've had enough; I can't eat another bite.* It was then I told her, *well, you should be full; you ate yours and most of mine."* We laughed many times over the years when we shared that story. There were many times over the *Drive of Faith* that neither of us had all we wanted to eat or enjoy, but God had given me a wife who never complained. She accepted life as it came to us; this is vital and important for any young people who wish to be involved in a *Drive of Faith;* be sure you get a mate who is willing to make sacrifices with you.

One evening after work with the crew in Erie, the yen to be home with Doris was more than I could handle. On this particular evening, I knew there would be a ride the next morning back to Erie, but there was no way home to Westfield. The railroad had posted a 20MPH sign for the trains crossing where our crew was stationed and working. I knew the rails went right through Westfield, so I jumped a freight car and rode the 40 miles or so. Trouble appeared when we approached Westfield; the train had been picking up speed since leaving Erie. It was probably doing about 80MPH when we came to Westfield. I felt it slow down and saw a sign telling the engineer not to exceed 60MPH. I thought to myself, t*his train is going all the way to Buffalo* (another 50 miles) *before it goes any slower.* I had to make a quick decision if I expected to get home that night.

The car I was riding was about the third or fourth car behind the engine. I swung out on the ladder, ready to jump when the engineer saw me and hollered loudly, waving for me to get back. I did not listen to him, watched for a place where there were no huge rocks or barriers, and jumped. To this day, I believe angels were there to curl me up with my knees to my chest and land me on my shoulders, rolling me down the embankment of fist size rocks and standing me up in the field below. It was amazing; a very foolish thing to do, but saved by the grace of God. How many times on this *Drive of Faith* I have been aware of supernatural help coming from an unexpected direction just in time.

I proceeded to walk out to Route 20 and start for home, about 4 miles from where I jumped. A police car saw me, asked for identification, heard my story, and bid me farewell. I am not sure if someone picked me up and gave me a ride into town or not, but I made it home. Needless to say, Doris was praising God with me when she heard my story. I think she must have appreciated my efforts to be with her on a lonely night.

One day a steel crew joined us at the Peach Street site to lay the girders and bolt the rails. They had a small trailer that housed a coal furnace to provide power and coals for the red hot bolts. They asked our crew if there was a man who wanted an extra $10 who would get up early the next morning and fire up the furnace so it would be ready for action at 7 AM when they arrived. I volunteered for the lucrative task and listened as they explained what I was to do the next morning. I rose early, stirred the fire they had banked for the night, opened the drafts, shoveled on the coal, and watched. 6:30 and then 6:40 came, but the steam pressure was still not up to par. I opened more drafts and worked the fire, when suddenly the steam pressure took off.

It came to the desired pressure but kept right on going. I shut the drafts and tried to slow the fire down but it kept right on climbing. It got so high that I thought it would surely blow up, so I went up on the bridge and waited for it to explode wondering how I would ever face the steel crew when they arrived. They had not explained and I did not know that the furnace had a safety feature that would blow off and make a loud whistle. While I am sitting there on the bridge (a boy of 17), going over my troublesome thoughts, the whistle goes off. I jumped: it scared me for a moment until I realized what it was. A sigh of relief left my lungs. Without telling anyone what happened, I presented the furnace with pressure up to par, and collected my booty. I have had many other scares on this *Drive of Faith,* and what a relief has come so many times just when you thought life was all over.

Doris and Russell

August 1, 1943

Chapter 20

A Holy Ghost College Discovered

After our marriage on August 1, 1943, we sought the Lord for a way to continue our education and prepare us for the ministry heaven had planned for our lives. We knew we could not return to Eastern as they did not allow students to marry during their three years at the college, so we made no effort to apply. I do not remember where we saw the advertisement or article about an interdenominational college with the word *Grace* in the title, but we contacted them and made application. It seems to me it was somewhere in Ohio or a neighboring State. We must have been accepted as we started to pack and make preparation for the move.

Our precious pastor, Rev. Nelson J. Kenyon, heard about this and talked to us. He made a contact with Zion Bible Institute at 846 Broadway in East Providence, RI. He got applications for us and we sent the papers in. Amazingly, we were accepted at that late date (close to September 1) and in no time were on a bus headed for Rhode Island. Pastor Kenyon was an adamant Assembly of God credential holder and wanted us in an Assembly college, but since that was impossible at that time because of our marriage and the fact that we had no money to pay tuition, room and board, he did the next best thing and got us accepted at Zion.

Before I tell you of our arrival, it is important for you to know why God orchestrated our path from Eastern Bible Institute to Zion Bible Institute in 1943. Eastern was rock solid in doctrine and gave us a good education during our first year. We could never say negative things concerning our year in the college; we deeply appreciate the foundation they gave us. The entire college staff were gems, caring for us students, educating us, and offering discipline and advice when necessary. In my mind, they were giants of the faith; President Allen Swift and his wife as the Dean of Women, to Walter Beuttler, Brothers Arnold and Buckwalter, Sister Bankirk, and many others.

However there was very little encouragement for students to move out in spiritual worship. There were only two people among the one hundred plus students who danced in the Spirit during the year we were there, and one of those was Doris Rosen. Only one person received the Baptism of the Holy Spirit and his name was Russell Pier. There were few messages in tongues and a strict rule enforced against more than three messages in a service. We never saw any of our teachers move in the Spirit during worship and only President Swift gave interpretations; that is as I remember it; being so many years ago I may have easily forgotten.

The divine plan of the Almighty is often difficult to understand in our day to day experience because the future is seldom revealed.

Why was God placing a 17 year old farm boy from western New York State in a Pennsylvania college to finish his high school education and meet a 21 year old gal from New Jersey for his soul mate?

Why did God arrange for this couple to marry and transfer from the Pennsylvania college to a different college in Rhode Island?

You may understand the last question better when you read part of the story of Zion Bible Institute; a College that had such a direct effect on our ministry and the future of this *Drive of Faith*. We received a spiritual education in Zion that was the corner stone of Faith School of Theology at its origin. It all began with a little lady from British Guiana in the early 20th century named Christine A. Gibson. Here are three of the many stories she told in our classes or chapel services. The details may be slightly off but I am writing these as I remember each one.

As a young woman she arrived at 846 Broadway in East Providence, RI, at a Faith Home that was under foreclosure. This home was a 2 ½ story building that had a dire need for paint. The grass around it was knee high.

Sister Gibson lay across the bed crying out to God when He personally gave her the words of Psalm 48:2; *Beautiful for situation, the joy of the whole earth, is mount Zion.* She arose from the bed, and with Bible in hands, she marched 7 times around the home in knee deep grass, proclaiming the words of Psalm 48:2. *Beautiful for situation, the joy of the whole earth, is mount Zion.*

That act of faith was realized in the fall of 1924 when the *School of the Prophets* (to become a few years later, Zion Bible Institute) opened its doors. Dedicated men and women, regardless of their financial condition, were given an opportunity to study God's Word and carry the Gospel to the ends of the earth. There is hardly a place on the globe that Zion graduates have not preached the unsearchable riches of Christ. Beloved, I owe any success in ministry to that woman of God who under His direction trained me in 1943-1945. I watched her and her staff live a life of faith that inspired me to become a leader in this *Drive of Faith.*

Among the things she taught me were stories like this when she listened to the Holy Spirit. During the 1930s it became necessary to build a dormitory between the Faith Home and the Tabernacle. It had been suggested that Zion apply for a construction loan of several thousand dollars from the local bank. The entire Board of the Faith Home Trustees met in the bank's office on a given date to sign and finalize the loan. The bank officials were present when all of a sudden one of Zion's board members broke out with a message in tongues.

Sister Gibson explained to the bank men that God had just made it clear she was not to sign for the loan. She offered to pay for any work the bank had done to prepare for that day and then she and the others from the school left for home. When they got back and explained what happened, Sister Thompson, a dear saint who worked for years at Zion, told Sister Gibson that God had been dealing with her. She had some savings set aside and gave it freely to construct the dormitory. There was great rejoicing in the camp as we listened to our leader reiterate that story several years later in a chapel service. This is another step in my learning experience on this *Drive of Faith* to give ear to the voice of God at any time and any place.

Chapter 21

An Education Begins at the Holy Ghost College

In those days no one was turned away from Zion for lack of finances and we for sure had none. I doubt if we had more than twenty dollars in our pockets when we arrived at 846 Broadway. I do not remember any details of the long Greyhound Bus trip from Westfield, NY, to Providence, RI. There were no Interstate Highways in those days and the speed limits were much lower than these days. I do remember arriving in Providence, getting onto an electric trolley, and arriving at six-points in East Providence in the early evening. We carried our suitcases a block or two to the college.

At that time the buildings on campus consisted of a Faith Home, a ladies dorm, a tabernacle which housed the men on the first floor, and the Grace More dorm where ladies, staff, and married couples lived over a large garage for the staff's vehicles. A female staff member showed us to our room in the Grace More dorm building. Doris and I walked through the door and immediately climbed wide wooden stairs facing us. Doris noticed the dust on the stairs but said nothing. At the top of the stairs we turned right to follow the hall. The first room on our right housed two male staff members and the room on our left had six lady students. Our room was the second on the right and the bathroom that served the whole dorm was on the left. The last room on the right before the outside stairway was inhabited by another married couple, while four lady students had the last room on the left.

When we opened the door to the place we would spend the next two years, an interesting sight met our eyes. On our left was a double white iron bed with chipped paint. On our right was a caned chair with a broken seat. Ahead of us by the double windows was a chest of drawers with one broken drawer hanging out. There was a small closet waiting for our suit and dresses to the right of the bed. I do not remember what the curtains looked like but I am sure they were not too impressive. We said nothing to the one who left us there, but when they were gone, Doris' first words were, *Russell, you got to get me out of here.* It was late and getting dark outside so I persuaded her to wait out the night. We had arrived on a Saturday evening; I do not remember where and what we had for breakfast, but at eleven o'clock we made our way to the church service. From the opening song to the end of powerful preaching, we could sense God's Spirit like neither of us had ever experienced before. The first opportunity Doris had, she spoke these words, *"Russell, this is what I have been looking for all of my life."*

It is impossible to tell in words how important our move to Zion Bible Institute in 1943 was to our future ministry. There were few other places in the country where the Holy Spirit demonstrated among the body of Christ in New Testament fashion. During our brief two year stay we witnessed all nine of the Gifts of the Holy Spirit in action. We were taught how to live day by day with faith in God for our natural provision. Our leaders demonstrated a holy life by the way they lived; we learned the value of proper daily appearance for all saints and especially those in the ministry; why certain entertainments were not conducive to holy living; the art of loving and serving those in need; and dozens of other behaviors that have been important in this *Drive of Faith.*

Beyond all of those vital matters mentioned above, we learned to obey the Holy Spirit and move as He directed. Our teachers encouraged us to make use of any Gift the Holy Spirit placed in our lives. Personally, as I yielded myself, the Holy Spirit granted me my first exercise of the Gift of Unknown Tongues, Interpretation of Unknown Tongues, Prophetic utterances, casting out of demons, animated demonstrations in the Spirit, hands on the sick and afflicted and seeing them healed, and other such New Testament spiritual activity. I learned these things from certain teachers at Zion and they laid a foundation that has never left.

It was common in our classes at Zion to have the Holy Spirit speak to us through Tongues, Interpretation, or Prophecy. As mentioned before, demonstrations in the Spirit took place that left an indelible impression on our hearts. Among dozens of times we witnessed these, I have never forgotten one that happened during a Sunday service. Evangelist Arthur Bristol, a Zion graduate of the late '30s, was visiting the college. During the meeting he arose from his seat in the congregation talking in other tongues. He walked up the aisle and across the front of the church about half way. He stopped, took off his suit jacket and threw it in an empty seat in the front row. Still talking in tongues for about 10 seconds, he reached down, picked up his jacket, and put it on. He then ran down the further aisle. When he walked across the back of the church, he started jumping up and down. After this, still talking in tongues, he walked up the aisle and took his seat.

Our college president, Christine Gibson, arose on the platform and standing there gave the interpretation which went something like this; *Stop your struggling with the works of the flesh, put off the old man* (demonstrated with taking off the coat) *with its evil deeds, seek the face of God. Now put on the new man* (demonstrated by putting the coat back on) *and you will be able to run through a troop and leap over a wall* (quoting from the Old Testament). *Victory will be sure when you follow God's directions.*

One Friday night before students left for Christmas break in 1943, the college had a social time. During that evening each class was to present their own unique program of poems, stories, etc. Our junior class chose Doris to chair a committee at which time she proposed a drama. She wrote it and chose various class members to take part. The actors chosen enacted the story of the birth of Jesus beautifully with a special scene at the end depicting Mary (played by Evelyn Crandall – cousin of Dr. Ben Crandall) and Joseph and a little baby (a life-like doll was used). As Mary spoke these words:

> *My soul doth magnify the Lord, And my spirit hath rejoiced in God my Saviour. For he hath regarded the low estate of his handmaiden: for, behold, from henceforth all generations shall call me blessed. For he that is mighty hath done to me great things; and holy is his name.*

Our class had prayed earnestly that God would make this play a blessing to everyone. Evelyn was so in the Holy Ghost that when she began that Scripture, *My soul doth magnify the Lord,* heaven dropped down in that college dining room where we were all assembled. Some fell prostrate under the power in His presence while the whole crowd arose and shouts of praise ascended in copious harmony. None of those present will ever forget the blessing of that night. This reminds me from time to time on this *Drive of Faith* that God can touch a simple thing and bring tremendous blessing.

Some other things happened at Zion in the after services around the altar that are worthy of mention. One was with my dear friend, Joel Whipple. My classmate, Jack Mitchell, and I were praying with Joel that he might receive the Baptism of the Holy Spirit. After a significant amount of waiting before God, Joel got disgusted because the Lord did not seem to answer and fill him with the Holy Spirit. Jack and I tried to encourage him, but he was really upset with God. He got up and started for the back of the tabernacle with the two of us following. Suddenly he stopped, mad at God he turned with doubled up fists to lay out both Jack and me. He froze on the spot and could not move. Standing there like a statue, he broke out in tears recognizing God had stopped him. We prayed with him and he left in good spirits. Joel was always a good friend while I was at Zion.

Russel and Doris Pier

Chapter 22

Demons Go, Miracles Happen, God Provides

Among the students at Zion Bible Institute in 1943 was a fine young man who was plagued with epilepsy; in those days effective medication had not been perfected. A seizure could overtake him at any time; the dinner table, doing duty of sweeping a floor, in chapel; anywhere, anytime. The man's head would begin to turn and eyes roll back, then sudden stiffness, etc. He would be carried out while students started praying. It was easy for anyone with spiritual perception to know that demon power was present, such as that demonstrated in the Gospels when Jesus confronted the epileptic in Matthew 17. Let me take a moment to explain. This was a saved young man that loved the Lord. A demon did not possess him; at times he was perfectly normal. Demons attacked a physical condition in his being that brought on those epileptic seizures. No one would know when this would happen unless the Holy Spirit revealed it.

As chef, I was in the kitchen one morning when the epileptic young man was sweeping the dining room. He saw the school buyer coming with his arms full of groceries. He held the kitchen door open for the buyer, but the kitchen door remained open. I noticed this out of the corner of my eye and turned to see if another person was coming with food. When I looked, I saw the young man holding the door and his head and eyes were turning as he started into a spell. I was about 12 feet from the door; I ran quickly, grabbed the young man by his shoulders and shouted his name, saying, *In the name of Jesus!* He came out of the spell immediately and was a little bit aggravated with me, saying, *what's the matter?* He was unaware of the spell taking hold of him.

There were two other experiences I remember about this brother with epilepsy; they happened in the sanctuary. The first took place on a day given to fasting and prayer. Many of the students had left the auditorium; there were probably about 20 or so left and no faculty or staff were present. A few were kneeling at the front seats and some of us were sitting prayerfully quiet, a few rows back from the front. There was a choir loft built on the first floor to the left of the stage. Two or three male students were sitting on the first step of the loft, including the young man subject to epilepsy. My wife was sitting on my right, next to the aisle, and a colleague, Jack Mitchell, was on my left. Jack poked me quick and pointed at the young man's head which was beginning to turn with eyes rolling back. At that moment with her eyes closed, Doris arose from her seat running, talking in tongues, toward the epileptic. Jack and I ran with her, and the three of us rebuked the epileptic spirit and immediately the young man came out of his seizure.

Quickly, Doris turned and started across the front of the church to a young woman of the same ethnic background as the epileptic, who was writhing on the floor, fighting off a seizure for the first time in her life. Immediately she was set free. Fearfully shaking, she thanked us for helping her. From this we learned that spirits can leap from one to another; this gave us a real education for our *Drive of Faith* in which we would several times meet demonic influence in the lives of believers under our care.

The second sanctuary incident happened toward the end of the school year on a Sunday afternoon. There were two in our graduating class who did not have the Baptism of the Holy Spirit, one of which was Melvin Hooper, a student from Bucksport, ME. About a dozen men and three or four ladies gathered in the sanctuary with Melvin to pray for his baptism. The brother subject to epilepsy was among us. Melvin and several of us men were seated on the floor near the altar.

Suddenly, several of us sensed a struggle going on in the spirit world. Melvin Hooper, one of our senior classmates was seeking for the Baptism of the Holy Ghost. Several students were gathered around him; among them was the epileptic. Suddenly many of us noticed (without saying a word) that a spiritual conflict was present. One brother moved himself so his body was between Melvin and our dear brother subject to epilepsy. All of us began quietly and some silently praying. At that point, Brother Rupert, our Dean of Men, came up from his apartment which was directly below the altar area where we were praying for Melvin. Brother Rupert looked the situation over and spoke to us students, advising those who wanted to pray for the brother subject to epilepsy to go down stairs with him and let the others stay and pray for Melvin. Brother Rupert's words to us were, *I could sense a spiritual struggle going on in my apartment down stairs, so I came up to see what was going on.*

Three or four of the young men took our brother subject to epilepsy and started down stairs. The brother did not understand why he had to go down stairs; he was completely oblivious to what was happening around him in the spirit world. To understand what took place you will need a description of the physical setting. It was a long aisle to the back of the sanctuary where there were two sets of double doors with a space of about six feet between them. An eight foot foyer met one coming from the auditorium which emptied into two sets of stairs, one to the left and one to the right. These stairways were broken by a landing half way down which made the stairs turn ninety degrees and proceed to the first floor.

The men with our epileptic brother had gone part way down the stairs to that landing. Unexpectedly my classmate, Lloyd Sharp, arose from where he was praying with Melvin and ran, speaking in tongues, to the back of the auditorium and into the foyer. Suddenly, with no one within twenty feet from him, Lloyd was picked up as if by invisible hands and thrown onto the floor. At that moment, the Spirit of the Lord came upon me and I raced (I do not remember my feet touching the floor, but I'm sure they did) down the middle aisle and through the right hand double doors. I leaped straddle with my legs over Lloyd and commanded the demonic spirit to take hands off my brother. The brothers on the landing with our epileptic brother turned to watch what was happening. Immediately Lloyd was set free, arose and came back with me to pray for our brother, Melvin, and the Baptism of the Holy Spirit. This was another experience that has helped me along this *Drive of Faith* when dealing with demonic spirits that occasionally attack believers.

While at ZBI I learned the value of personal messages given by the Holy Spirit. Elijah, Elisha, Nathan, Ahijah, and many others were used of God to bring messages to individuals in the Old Testament. In the New Testament Ananias, Agabus, Paul and others unnamed were anointed by the Holy Ghost to speak words of comfort and warning to individuals. This has been invaluable on this *Drive of Faith.*

In the spring of 1944 I received a letter from President Roosevelt telling me to appear in two weeks from the date of that mailing for induction into the United States Army. The doctors had already approved me and I was ready to answer the call to arms. The government had not yet approved Zion Bible Institute as an institution for training ministers, therefore its male students could not be deferred. One afternoon, my wife and I laid the letter before the Lord and prayed for God's direction. We felt we should finish our education, but if God felt different about it, we were ready to obey Him and go fight for our country's freedoms.

To my knowledge, no one else knew about the letter that came that day. Suddenly Floyd Green from the senior class began walking up and down in the hall outside our room, talking in tongues. He was not shouting but he was not very quiet; we could hear him plainly in our room. After five or ten minutes of this, we opened the door of our room to see what was going on. Immediately, Floyd, speaking under the unction of the Holy Spirit said, *I don't know what is going on with you two, but God says to call those things that are as though they are not.* Doris and I began to rejoice together in faith, believing God for the impossible. It was two or three days later that the school lawyer came to tell us that the college had just been approved by the government for the deferment of its male students. Brother Green was often used to speak words from the Spirit to various individuals.

Another time when a personal message helped my wife and me came during the closing week of our senior year. Our class had gathered for an all-night of prayer. Brother Arnold Waring, our class advisor, was with us and before we dismissed to leave, he had us all sit down in a couple of rows and began to pray for each of us. Doris and I were the first ones he laid hands on, and when he did, he began to prophesy.

We knew what each male student in the class was going to be doing after graduation; Ben and Jeanne were going to NYC to work with his mother in a mission; class president, Lloyd Sparks was chosen as pastor in Brocton, MA; Melvin was going back to Maine with a tent to preach tent revivals; Jack was going to Canada for evangelistic services; and all the other men and some of the ladies had places of ministry, while Doris and I had no divine direction as yet. Bro. Waring's first words to us were, *It is none of your business what other people are doing.* We laughed together as we listened to the message encouraging us about the future. It was beautiful and came out just as he prophesied.

One more incident happened in the closing week of school. Two of my classmates had been keeping company for several months. They had made plans to wed and minister together, when they were suddenly rebuked and separated by a message in tongues from one of our teachers who was often used in that gift. From my understanding, the mother of the young man felt the young lady he was about to marry was below his social class and wanted someone better for her son. The mother shared her feelings with this teacher who used her gift of tongues to rebuke and separate the two. This caused the young couple a lot of weeping and praying as neither of them wanted to disobey the Lord. They had prayed for months and felt at peace and assured that God had put them together for their life's work.

Within a day or two, Pastor George Shea of Rochester, NY, the convention speaker for our graduation, met this broken couple in the hall of Faith Home. He knew nothing of what had happened; he was a complete stranger to the couple. He walked up to them, placed their hands together, and prophesied of their future happiness and ministry which would last for several decades. This event taught me a powerful lesson and further prepared me to be a leader in this *Drive of Faith.* I had the joy of being with this couple years later in New York State where they pastored most of their lives.

Chapter 23

Chosen, Embarrassed, and Blessed

In early September, 1944, our Dean of Men, Bro. Rupert, had a revelation during the noon meal in the dining hall. His eyes were closed while he was praying within when God spoke to his heart to begin evening prayers with seven students; earnest praying for a revival and a special move of the Holy Spirit. Suddenly he was shown in his spirit where these seven were seated at various tables but was not told their names. When he opened his eyes and looked, he had seen my wife and me among that group. I am not sure who all seven were, but I do remember Pearl Coffin and Sister Stewart (an older black student – late 20s or early 30s). There were three others and their names may come to me before I finish this article.

Bro. Rupert came to each of us privately and told us what he saw, asking if we would meet each evening in his apartment for a season of prayer. We all agreed and began some of the most intense praying I have ever heard. As a result, things began to happen. Balls of fire fell in the local barroom between drunkards and they would take off running to Zion's Tabernacle where they fell at the altar crying out for mercy. People were getting healed and demons were cast out. Our prayer group did not take any credit but we kept on faithfully meeting for prayer each night for three or four weeks.

Our college president, Sister Gibson, felt to attend the funeral of Amy Simple McPherson in California during this time. She left a very godly woman, our precious Sister Luna Blanchard in charge of the college. The events of Friday evening are not clear in my memory, so I will simply state the things I know. The authorities called a meeting on Friday evening in the dining hall to consider whether or not the college should have a day of fasting and prayer. The prayer group went to the Dean of Men's apartment, as they had been doing for weeks. Bro. Rupert was away that evening but left his apartment open as he had on other nights when he could not be present. We were well into intercessory prayer when someone came to the apartment door and told us we were wanted downstairs in the dining room where they were all gathered. Reluctantly we left and started down the wide stairs leading to the dining room doors. When we were half way down, suddenly the Holy Spirit came upon my wife and she began speaking powerfully in other tongues and pointed back to the apartment. Immediately we returned to the apartment and continued in intercessory prayer.

For one reason or another, some of the staff felt the prayer group was forming a rebellion against the authority of the college. The Friday night gathering in the dining room broke up and we heard nothing more until Saturday morning. All the students and staff of the college gathered again in the dining room and one or more of our teachers spoke about Korah and his gang who rebelled against Moses. One teacher suggested those who were standing with Sister Blanchard gather around her and those who disagreed could stand back. Our prayer group members were some of the first to show we were devoted to Sister Blanchard and the leadership of the college; none of us had even the slightest thought of insurrection or disobedience.

The same teacher that had split that couple up in the closing paragraphs of the last chapter, suddenly came to my wife. She took hold of her shoulders and while talking loudly in tongues, and shook her violently. The shaking was so forceful that the buttons ripped off the front of her blouse exposing a small part of her slip and bra to the whole student body. My wife and I fell to our knees weeping; mostly because we did not understand. We knew there was not a rebellious spirit of any kind in our bones; that God had chosen us to be intercessors and we were just doing what we had been doing each night; praying for the college we loved.

There was no interpretation to the message in tongues and so everyone just sat reverently. Eventually the service was dismissed and we all left for our rooms. My wife threw herself on the bed with her face to the wall while I sat in a chair quietly thinking and praying. Suddenly the Holy Spirit gave

Doris the Scripture in 1 Kings 21:4: *And he laid him down upon his bed, and turned away his face, and would eat no bread.* God's Holy Spirit said directly to her, *Now, turn yourself, go eat your dinner in the dining room and live!* We both obeyed the Spirit and continued our lives as though nothing had happened.

When Sister Gibson returned from the funeral and the story of that morning was related to her, she called Doris and me to her rooms. She assured us that it would not have been that way if she had been present. She complimented us for the spirit we had shown through it all. This event had a tremendous effect on our lives, preparing us for the *Drive of Faith.*

We had many wonderful experiences and a great spiritual education at Zion Bible Institute. We learned that one did not have to be popular, well known, or have an outgoing personality to be used of God. In the Faith Home there was a dear sister by the name of Annie Bucklin. She was a blessing to so many. She was one among the half a dozen elderly people Sister Gibson had given a home to where she lived herself. I do not know what Sister Bucklin's responsibilities were; perhaps she helped peel potatoes or other small chores in the Faith Home. She was always in church; a very unobtrusive individual that few would pay much attention to.

Her ministry was a powerful encouragement to those who were depressed. I had been cooking all day in the institute kitchen and was standing by the door pressing the button and ringing the bell for students and staff to come down to supper. I was tired and often wondered what I was doing there when I felt the burden to preach. At that moment, Annie came by. When she saw me, she stopped and said quietly, Brother Pier, I have a Scripture for you; *Be not weary in well doing, for in due season you will reap if you faint not.* That sent me to 7th heaven in my spirit and made my day. To think that God had talked to someone like Annie and told her to give me that Word; it was unbelievable.

On another occasion Annie was used to encourage our friend, Amy Springer. Amy was a student and on one Sunday morning had been used by God to give her first interpretation in the church service. Like most of us, Amy had been attacked by the enemy with thoughts; *you know that was yourself, etc. etc. etc.* That Sunday afternoon Amy was coming down the steps from the church when Annie was ascending. They met part way and Annie Bucklin turned to Amy and said, *Amy, I have a Scripture for you; John was in the Spirit on the Lord's Day.* Annie knew nothing of the struggle within Amy's mind about the interpretation that morning. Over and over again, Annie was used like that to bring a Word from the Bible to someone in need. This has helped me in this *Drive of Faith,* to teach others that:

- There are hurting people everywhere.
- Any Spirit filled believer can prophesy a Word from the Bible [1 Cor. 14:31].
- One does not have to be important in the church – any unobtrusive Annie can reach out to others if she wants to.

Annie Bucklin had invited my wife and me to her room in the Faith Home several times. We finally decided to take her up on the invitation and told her we would come about 7 that evening. After a half hour of interesting and inspiring conversation, we rose to depart. But Annie said, *Please have prayer with me before you go.* We agreed and knelt to pray one by one. Now there was no way for Annie to know that Doris and I had used our last sliver of hand soap that morning, but when we were ready to say our good byes, Annie said, *By the way, do you folk need some soap?* Not willing to tell our needs to anyone so God could always get the glory for our provision, we replied, *why do you ask?* Immediately she went to the bottom drawer of her dresser and pulled out 3 bars of soap and said, *while I was praying a few minutes ago, I saw 3 bars of soap float by my eyes, and I just feel like you have a need.* Needless to say, we went back to our room rejoicing in a God who cares enough about His children to provide even small details like hand soap. It was another important lesson in this *Drive of Faith*: God is concerned about little things.

Chapter 24

Lessons in Preaching, Spiritual Manifestations, and Faith

Late in the spring of 1944 Dr. Leonard Heroo, our Homiletics 2 teacher appointed each member of the junior class a speaking assignment. Eastern Bible Institute did not teach any speaking subjects during the freshman year, while all of our classmates at Zion had already had Homiletic 1. My wife took this assignment in stride as she had spoken to the youth service in her church a few times. Me? I had but one experience to remember and it was the biggest flop of the century. And now, I was to get up in front of my Homiletic teacher and the whole class and preach a 10 or 15 minute sermon. Dr. Heroo had taught us how to outline a message and gave us one admonition that was vital to me; practice, practice, practice, and practice some more.

I prayed desperately for God's advice for a text. He led me to Matt. 7:13-14; Enter ye in at the strait gate: for wide is the gate, and broad is the way, that leadeth to destruction, and many there be which go in thereat: Because strait is the gate, and narrow is the way, which leadeth unto life, and few there be that find it. Once I had an outline on paper I went anywhere I could find alone and preached. The boys had told me of a place they termed as Preacher's Rock, about a mile from the college out in the woods. After I found it, I went there more than once and preached to the birds and leaves while they sang and clapped for me. I do not know how many times I practiced; perhaps a dozen or more before I felt ready for the task. Doris spoke on her assigned day which was previous to mine. She did a great job; I think she preached her sermon, Wanted, a Man, from the Book of Ezekiel.

When my day came, Doris was so nervous for me that she left the room. I think she may have been listening in the hall just out of sight but I am sure she felt I might bomb out and fail. I walked to the pulpit in confidence, and let it rip. It was hell fire and brimstone to my class who I pictured as an evangelistic crowd of sinners. The Lord helped me depict a broad highway with millions of drunkards, smokers, harlots, proud and lost sinners enraptured in their pleasures, headed for a precipice they refused to acknowledge. The message pictured each sinner as they plunged over the abyss into hungry flames of torture. From there I returned to the crossroads that divided the broad and narrow. I discovered a little low gate in a wall. I pushed on it, but it would not open. The class watched as I knelt and prayed the sinner's prayer and suddenly without a touch the gate automatically opened for my passage. A straight and narrow path was seen stretching from the penitent sinner to a city of lights. On the path were thousands (nowhere near as the millions on the broad way) singing, praying, and enjoying life to the fullest as they walked in the Spirit.

To be very honest, my memory does not recall any accolades from my teacher, class, or wife. Believe me, for some reason it is lost in the past. What I do vividly remember is Dr. Heroo's choices of the two best junior and senior preachers to represent their class in a Sunday night service of Zion Gospel Tabernacle. One female and one male were appointed from each class. I would only be guessing who the senior speakers were, but Evelyn Crandall (cousin to Dr. Ben Crandall, former president of Zion Bible College) was chosen from our junior class. She was a polished speaker and well liked. When Dr. Heroo breathed out my name as the male speaker, I nearly fell over. Again, I wish I could remember my wife's reactions, but nothing comes to mind. This experience in this *Drive of Faith* caused me to live and do my work to the best of my ability regardless of what others thought. In the end, it would be God who rewards and gives the final, *Well Done*.

Sunday night arrived. Our President, Christine Gibson, homiletics teacher, Dr. Heroo, and four or five other teachers were on the platform. Between 2 and 3 hundred people were stretched out in front of us. To my amazement, seniors preached first, followed by Miss Crandall of the junior class. After she finished, Dr. Heroo did something I shall never forget; something I assure you as a public speaking and homiletics teacher I would never do. He meant no harm but I was never sure why he did it. He introduced me with words similar to this; *Ladies and gentlemen, we have with us tonight one of the coming generation's great evangelists; allow me to introduce to you our junior male speaker: Russell Pier.* I nearly died. But this was no time for a funeral. People were waiting to hear God's Word. What a lesson this was in this *Drive of Faith.* It has been something else when facing hundreds of different churches, camp meetings, and special events to be introduced with words I never felt I deserved; such times need to humble us rather than the opposite.

Zion Bible Institute was a college where one could expect manifestations of the Holy Spirit most any time of the day or night and most anywhere on campus. One interesting day, just before the 11 AM chapel service, the presence of the Lord was erupting in the long, wide hall leading up to the sanctuary. The students were on their way to the service when suddenly the Spirit of God fell like rain on that long first floor hall way. Students were shouting, singing, dancing in the Spirit, and some lay prostrate on the floor. This was to be expected any time but read the following and smile.

Brother and Sister Ruppert (remember: he was the Dean of Men) had the first apartment on that floor. They were in their forties and had only been married a year or two. They had just recently brought their first and only week-old baby from the hospital. Brother Ruppert had gone to the train station that morning to pick up his mother-in-law who had never been in a Pentecostal meeting and knew nothing of spiritual matters. Brother Ruppert did not know the Holy Spirit was moving in the hall or he would not have brought his mother-in-law in the front door. The two of them had to walk at least 80 feet or more the whole length of the building to his apartment. He was really embarrassed as he tugged on her arm while she was trying to stop and observe what in the world was happening. His wife's mother knew her daughter had married a preacher but had no idea it was like this. She came to help her daughter with the new born baby and got a real taste of Pentecost while she was there. It turned out to be blessing to that whole family. One more lesson for me on the *Drive of Faith;* when God wants to do something, give Him room regardless of the presence of any personnel.

Sister Gibson tells the story from her early days when a certain middle-age couple of the higher class came to the Tabernacle service. As pastor, she desired everything to be just so. *Lord, keep everything in order as we want this couple to come again.* She was particularly concerned that Sister Edna did not get up with the tambourine and dance. But guess what happened? Edna got blessed when the music began, and away she went. She had long flowing hair that was done up in a bun; down it came on her back with hairpins on the floor. The new couple took it all in. When the service ended, Pastor Gibson shook hands with the couple and they assured her they were coming back. They became one of the long standing friends of Zion Bible Institute. It was actually the joy that Edna expressed in her dancing that made an impression on them. A great story that has helped me in this *Drive of Faith;* let God take care of His blessing and do not interfere with your human reasoning.

It was extremely important in this *Drive of Faith* that we learn how to trust God, and that begins with little things. Like the sliver of soap you read about when Little Annie came to our rescue, my double edge razor blades had diminished. I was trying to sharpen the last one by rubbing it in a dry drinking glass. After mentioning this to the Lord in prayer, I was blessed one evening by Shirley Bailey, a new male student who arrived from Lincoln, ME. We were good friends with his sister, Amy Springer, so I went with Shirley to his room. While unpacking his clothes, he pulled out a whole string of double edged razor blades. I gave him no reason to believe that I needed some, but as he went to put them in his drawer, he said, *do you need some razor blades? Someone gave me more than I need.* Needless to say, I was walking on air and praising God with each step as I left for my room that evening with enough blades to last a long time.

We were on our way to Providence, a little over a mile, to pick up our graduation pictures. The pictures were paid for, but we had no money for transportation. It cost eight cents per person, one way. We went through the Faith Home to check the mail, although we seldom received help by that method. No mail! There was nothing else to do but walk through difficult neighborhoods and get the pictures by shoe leather express. I had just put my hand on the front door handle at Faith Home to begin the journey, when a voice behind me said, *Russell, here is something to get your wife and you some ice cream or whatever.* One of my best friends and a teacher at Zion, pressed a fifty cent piece in my hand and hurried away. Hallelujah! One more lesson in this *Drive of Faith*.

It was Sunday and we used the last dab of tooth paste in the last tube we had. The Lord had never failed us, but it sure looked like it this time. Monday, Tuesday, Wednesday – no toothpaste! At the Wednesday night church service, Bro. Joel Whipple from Connecticut approached me. He was a good friend of ours and he gave me $20 with this message;

> *I was supposed to give you $10 Sunday night. But I failed the Lord, and now I doubled it. God bless you.*

After thanking him, I told him my story. We had used salt to clean our teeth with for three days; so I learned two things from this experience that have helped me tremendously in this *Drive of Faith*. First, improvise the best you can when help does not arrive. Second, others may suffer when you disobey God.

Beloved, it is much easier to trust Him for the thousands and millions, when you have found Him faithful to provide the change and dollar bills.

Chapter 25

Preparation for Greater Things

During World War Two, the United States Government demanded an acceleration of classes in the colleges where male students were classified as 4D and exempt from war detail. In 1944 this involved Zion after it received approval from the Attorney General's office to defer students until after their graduation. Our college president, Rev. Christine Gibson, asked our lawyer friend, Swan Messerlian, to explain this to the student body. We were all seated in the dining room and listening intently. Evidently there were members of the faculty who were hearing this for the first time as well as students. It had been rumored about the campus that male students that needed deferment would have to attend summer classes and there were pros and cons about the issue.

As Brother Messerlian began to explain the importance of summer classes, I noticed the husband of the teacher who shook my wife at that meeting about our so called rebellion back in chapter 23. He was one of the main teachers on the faculty and was not keen on staying on campus during the hot summer to teach. I saw him poke his wife on the leg and whisper something in her ear. A few seconds later, his wife rose, speaking in tongues, walked over to Brother Messerlian and in a rebuking tone finished her message, returned and sat down. Everything was quiet as no interpretation came. In a moment or two Sister Gibson spoke up and said, *"I'm not sure what this message is about. I asked Bro. Messerlian to explain this to all of us"*. Well, when she said that, I saw the speaker in tongues look down and her husband dropped his jaw. It appeared that both of them did not know authority had come from the top. After that episode, everyone listened and questions were answered as the meeting came to a close. It has helped me in this *Drive of Faith* to know that some people try to use the gifts God has given them for their own agenda; this has been invaluable to me.

That was a hot summer as day after day my wife and I and several others attended classes. There were no air conditioners in the classrooms or dormitories. I remember opening the books to study in the afternoons while the sweat ran off my brow. Subjects were taught only to juniors and seniors. I have no idea how the administration gave us all credits for a full year when we were only taught 3 months. Those taking junior courses went into the senior class that fall and we seniors were finished with our education but returned the next spring for graduation. In other words, we were credited with a whole year of education after only three months of summer classes.

The summer school helped me in my *Drive of Faith* in two ways. First, it caused me to strictly follow curriculum credits when I set up the college in Maine and second, it helped me see that students could study under difficult weather situations when necessary. Our first winter in the new campus at Brooklin, ME, was brutal and students endured difficult circumstances during that year of their education.

I became the head chef at Zion while my senior class attended their senior year as students; I was 19 years old, cooking for 120 students and staff. I had several opportunities for ministry but received a red light from heaven on each one. It was difficult to understand at that time; chosen as class speaker, opportunities for ministries offered, but stay at college and cook? I did not have the slightest idea that Sister Gibson would ask me to teach at Zion 9 years later, and 12 years later a revelation would come from heaven to open a Bible college in the State of Maine. It was in the kitchen that I learned what I needed to know to properly administrate a *faith* Bible college for many decades. We prayed in food, learned to take the heat, had pastry cooks, dishwashers, waitresses, helpers, etc., to oversee. I learned how to get along with difficult people and many other things that have helped me immensely on this *Drive of Faith*. Frugality and proper economic use of God's provisions was another important part of my training during those years in the kitchen at Zion.

After graduation from Zion in 1945, I stayed and cooked for the summer staff. That summer Doris and I were able to open a store-front mission in the city of Pawtucket, about 5 miles from Zion. Some of my classmates held a DVBS for us. I remember Phyllis Stewart (Knudson) and Vivian Harris (Hammil) being among the children's workers. We continued this mission for about 4 months during which time an interesting event took place. It was one Saturday evening that a cadet nurse ventured inside and took a seat next to where my wife's Bible was. After playing the piano during the singing Doris went back and sat down by the pretty little dark-haired nurse. I was at the pulpit directing the service when she turned and asked my wife who that angelic looking person was on the platform. Doris told her that was her husband. I was a curly, black-haired, kid of 19. The cadet accepted the invitation to come to the altar and I led her to the Lord and prayed.

That nurse found the address of Zion and one day showed up to visit us. She was talking with us in our room when I adjusted the window which fell on my hand. Immediately she came to look at my hand to see if there was any injury and held it longer than I thought she needed to. From that time on, I was cautious to keep my distance when she came around. When she came to visit I attempted to find other things to do. After three or four visits, she had the audacity to say in private to Doris, *I can't figure you out, I'm in love with your husband, and you don't even seem to care.* Doris, in her cute little way, returned with an amiable quip, *No, let the best woman win.* When Doris told me later what she said, I made sure I was not around when she came to visit; and the visits stopped. This experience gave me insight that would help me in the training of men and women for Christian ministry in this *Drive of Faith.*

During the evenings of that summer's education at Zion (1944), several of the staff and students met at the altar in the Tabernacle. We learned how to intercede in prayer for four and five hours, prostrate on our stomachs, crying out to God for answers. As a result, things began to happen. I remember one night when a man came stumbling into the Tabernacle and fell at the altar to surrender his life to God. At the very time we were interceding for souls, he had been in a local tavern when a ball of fire out of heaven suddenly came down by his side, scaring him and others. He took to running and ended up at our altar to repent of his sins. I learned in this *Drive of Faith* that mighty things happen in response to intercessory prayer.

Another interesting thing happened at those prayer meetings. About twelve of us were worshipping one evening, standing in a circle when the power of God fell. It struck me in such a manner that I fell prostrate on my back and received what some call the *second blessing*. Others have different terms; *wholly sanctified, entire dedication, fully consecrated, etc.* I may not have realized it at the time, but something happened in my being that changed my life forever. It felt as though liquid fire filled my body. It was a sensation I shall never forget and my life was different after that experience. It helped me in this *Drive of Faith* when I wrote the Doctrine Two course for the college in Maine. Someone will ask, *Did you ever sin after that?* My answer has always been, *certainly, we are all subject to sinning because we live in a body that has not been redeemed.* The Apostle Paul wrote in Ephesians 1:13-14, *ye were sealed with that Holy Spirit of promise, Which is the earnest of our inheritance <u>until the redemption of the purchased possession</u>, unto the praise of His glory.* Our spiritual souls have been forgiven and redeemed from sin and that part of us will go to heaven when we die, but the body is not going to heaven without a translation when we are given a new body. So yes, we are still subject to sinning after being wholly sanctified, but we treat sin differently. All sin becomes putrid, filthy, and we hate it. Purity is a priority, something that is most important every day that we live.

This is a quote from my Doctrine 2 book: "Regeneration is a doctrine and so is sanctification. Sanctification is a definite word with a significant meaning. It is not repentance or regeneration or the new birth. Sanctification is a doctrine by itself, acknowledged by believers and taught by the Holy Scriptures. We must be careful not to take from the Bible this powerful, life-changing doctrine. Sanctification is just as distinct a teaching as the new birth and regeneration; it is not a vague, uncertain blessing, but an instantaneous work of the grace of God. Christ is made unto us wisdom, and righteousness, and sanctification, and redemption. Sanctification is a separate operation of the Holy Spirit in the heart of a believer already redeemed from his sin."

Chapter 26

Understanding the Work of the Holy Spirit

A nother powerful incident happened while I was at Zion Bible Institute that gave me real insight into the reception of the Baptism of the Holy Ghost. Swan Messerlian, who I have mentioned before, was a very dear friend of ours and the same to most everyone that knew him. Before He was saved, he was a rising star among the Democrats in politics; Swan was the President of the Young Democrats in Rhode Island. He was a trial lawyer. In the late 30s there were 13 men charged with gang rape in Rhode Island; Swan was the lawyer for number 12. The first 11 had been convicted and sentenced to prison. Swan walked into court and pleaded insanity for his client – won his case and the man was let go. The lawyer for the 13th saw what Swan did, followed suit and convinced the jury that found him not guilty (because of insanity).

Swan joined the staff of Zion a year or two before Doris and I arrived at the college. He did not have the Baptism of the Holy Spirit and was constantly seeking the same. He was so desperate that he followed whatever instructions anyone gave him, even to the extreme. One person he looked up to told him (while he was seeking at the altar) to raise his hands and praise the Lord and he would get filled. After spending a lengthy time at the altar with arms so tired he could no longer hold them up, he went to his room and propped his arms up with pillows as he lay on his bed. Brother Baker, a student, told Swan that would not work; God does not give His gifts for what we do, they come by faith.

Waiting for the supper bell to ring so we could all go down the wide stairs to the dining room, Swan was talking with Doris, Jack, and me, about the Baptism of the Spirit. Jack was sitting on the floor under the window and just at that moment the sheer curtain let go and fell covering Jack, who lifted his arms under the curtain and praised the Lord, proclaiming to Swan, *Here, Brother, this is the way it comes.* We all laughed and agreed that it just comes suddenly and sometimes we do not understand why.

One glorious night it happened. It was the closing spring convention of 1945; most everyone had left the altar leaving about 12 or 15 of us still hanging around. Brother Swan was prostrate on his back, lying quietly, waiting for the Baptism of the Holy Spirit. Brother Jack Mitchell was kneeling beside him. Suddenly I noticed Jack listening intently as he put his ear down closer to Swan. He looked over at me and beckoned me to come. I knelt down on the other side of Brother Swan and heard a very soft voice speaking words in a foreign language. I rushed to tell Sister Gibson who was standing in the back of the auditorium and the folk began to gather. Within 5 or 10 minutes about 50 people gathered as the news spread through the campus like wild fire. A crowd stood up on the platform looking down at Swan while others gathered round. Sister Gibson was talking in tongues and praising God in English as praises went up everywhere.

Suddenly Brother Swan opened his eyes and said in a quiet matter of fact tone, *I'm fooling all you people. I'm speaking a language but I don't feel a thing.* At that remark, Sister Gibson began by letting Swan know she felt the witness of the Spirit and all he needed to do was continue speaking the new language God had given him. *But,* he said, *I don't feel anything. This is so easy, I'm just fooling you all.* At that, Sister McClurg, a middle age missionary who had spent several years in China, interrupted. She said in strong affirmative words, *Swan, you have been speaking in 3 dialects of the Chinese language that I understand. You have been telling me answers to some questions I have been asking God about in my private prayer closet. This is the Holy Ghost on you.*

At that, Brother Swan closed his eyes as he said, *but I don't know why I don't feel something.* We all encouraged him to continue worshipping God with his new language. After a few moments, suddenly he shouted, *Oh, Oh, I feel something now. It is in my feet and coming up my legs.* The whole place broke out in a powerful move of the Holy Ghost; some were dancing and most were shouting praises as we watched this brother, a friend of everyone, being filled with the Holy Spirit. Swan Messerlian was up the whole night, praying with different ones to receive the Baptism of the Holy Spirit. When I came down to the kitchen around 7 o'clock, Swan had a man on his knees in the dining room praying. I do not know how many received at that time, but our Brother Swan was a changed man. Not long after that convention, the Davis Sisters in St. John, NB, Canada, called him to preach a revival. He went there that summer and the report I got was that over 50 people were filled with the Spirit in the couple of weeks he was there. He had such a simple way of encouraging people to believe a God who cannot lie to give them the Baptism of the Spirit.

The humility of such a great man to be personal friends with so many students helped me in the *Drive of Faith* to touch the personal lives of hundreds of students over the years. Even at this age (93) I make my advice and Christian friendship available to several who call, write, or text me often.

It was the Monday previous to my Saturday graduation in 1945 that Sister Gibson called me into her room to give me $25.00. It was to buy a new graduation suit. Doris and I had been praying but had told no one, as was and always will be our practice in this *Drive of Faith*. We made a trip to Providence, picked out a suit, and left it to be altered. The day before graduation we picked it up and God had done the miraculous for us again.

When we first arrived at Zion, I was very young – a month before I was 18. As any newlywed couple might do, we often walked around, hand in hand. One day Sister Gibson asked us to see her. In a very kind and graceful way, she explained that people outside of the campus would not know Doris and I were a married couple. She helped us see the importance of living above reproach to those who did not live with us on the campus. People on the outside needed to know that Zion was a *Bible* school, not a *Bridal* school. We were not offended in the least and always walked with our hands to the side after that when we were off campus. This helped me see how little things were important to portray a proper picture to others as I continued on this *Drive of Faith*.

There are many chapel incidents I might write about, but this one was rather unique and has never left my memory. It was on a Monday morning when chapel was held in the dining room. During testimonies, Brother Floyd Green rose from his seat and began to walk with footsteps that could be heard by everyone. Floyd, a senior, had often been used to give messages in tongues, interpretations, or prophesy; but this was different – usually loud and boisterous, Floyd was closed-mouth, only his footsteps could be heard. It was a moment or more when finally someone gave this interpretation (only part as I do not recall the whole); *Behold, the stately steppings of the Lord your God in the midst of His people.* If my memory serves me right, the remainder had something to do with what He sees, with what He might be grieved, and with what He rejoices over. I have been reminded from time to time on this *Drive of Faith* that God sees everything on our college campus and some of it may affect His attitude towards the needs of the people. His stately steppings can be heard if we want to listen.

One fasting and prayer chapel that has helped me tremendously on this *Drive of Faith* happened in the spring of 1944. Rev. Arnold F. Waring, one of our greatest teachers, was speaking. Doris and I both came from churches where we had been taught that 1 Cor. 14:27 meant there must never be more than 3 messages in tongues in a service. During this chapel service there were several; in fact, I began to count and had heard at least 13 while Rev. Waring was preaching. He had flowed so beautifully in the Holy Spirit, interpreting each message. Doris and I nudged each other, and without saying a word we were each thinking, *How can this be? The Bible says only 3.* At that very moment an interpretation came from Rev. Waring's mouth; *Some say 2 and some say 3, but God cannot be limited.* After that service, Doris and I began to study the text in 1 Cor. 14; *If any man speak in an unknown tongue, let it be by two, or at the most by three, and that by course; and let one interpret.*

This was a matter of concern for several days until Rev. Waring explained in class. He caused us to see, first, that the verse was in the midst of a corrective chapter where *people* and not gifts or demonstrations were being dealt with. Wives were not educated and did not always understand the speaker; they would ask their husbands who always sat on the opposite side of the church, what the speaker meant. More than one would try to give a message or prophecy at the same time. All of this was causing confusion and so were those who possessed the Gift of Tongues when they tried to give all the messages instead of allowing others to use their gift. As a result, Paul simply laid down instructions that limited the number of messages *one* person should be giving in a service. For better understanding, we might say, *If any man* (individual) *gives messages, let him limit himself to 2 (at the most 3), so that others might have an opportunity to use their gift. And then let someone else interpret so that testimony is given by 2 or 3 people,* 1 Cor. 14:27. This has been valuable to me in this *Drive of Faith.* I have always encouraged, both in my pastorates and in the college, the exercise of the Gift of Tongues and Interpretation; as Paul said, *Forbid not the speaking in tongues.*

Chapter 27

Transition Time: Life with John & Ann Messerlian

Early in the summer of 1945, Brother Swan came to me with a question; *"Have you been praying for a car?"* He was well aware of our financial condition and had helped us in small ways at different times. My answer was in the affirmative. He asked me to walk with him next door to the campus. He took me to a low building with room enough for about 3 vehicles. We found the building empty except for an older coup at one end that was up on blocks. Swan explained that the owner of the car died in the war during the fighting in Europe. His parents sold it to Brother Swan for $20. It had been there in storage for about 2 or 3 years and needed a new coil and battery. I changed the oil and pumped up the tires. I had never heard of the make and model – a 1931 Huppmobile coup. The inside was well taken care of but the outside was a real dull olive green. Doris and I bought paint and with brushes, painted the whole car black; it looked great when we finished.

Late that summer we decided to take a trip to New Jersey. We took our friend, Robert Steward, an underclassman and a family acquaintance of several years with Doris' family. The trip was filled with surprises. We had a couple of flat tires; bought patches and fixed them on the side of the road in Connecticut. The wheels were made so that the tires were mounted on a rim and if not handled correctly, the rim could spring off and injure one quite easily. What a lesson on this *Drive of Faith,* sitting on the side of a highway with the tube across my knee, gently spreading the glue for the patch, and applying the same to the rubber. In other words, learning a life's lesson of doing what you can with the little you have; not complaining, enjoying the blessings that He gives, living in victory. The tire is back on the car and we are coasting down another hill on the Merritt Parkway; coasting because the radiator is steaming while driving up the last hill and needs cooling off. We did that on several inclines but we made it safe into New Jersey to the home of Doris' parents. Uncle John Babbitt worked on the car the next day or two, taking care of the problem.

The old 31 Huppmobile made the return trip to Rhode Island and became a blessing for several months. One of our dearest friends, Sister Stewart, an Afro-Canadian, needed a ride to Boston to see her Bishop. Our colleague, Jack Mitchell, needed a ride to Boston to catch a bus going to his home in Maine. We could only get 3 in the front seat, so Brother Jack rode in the trunk with the door slightly ajar and Sister Stewart in the front seat with my wife. We often joked about it later on; what would we say if an officer stopped us; a preacher driving, another preacher going to see the Bishop, and the preacher we had in the trunk headed for a revival meeting in Maine? We have had to improvise many times on this *Drive of Faith* in order to be a blessing to others.

The fall of 1945 was the beginning of our transition from Zion's kitchen to full time ministry. I am trusting God to make this chapter a special blessing to young preachers who have graduated from college but have not yet found their niche. There were a lot of strange emotions, doubts, great questions for God, and periods of bewilderment during the next 12 months.

Winston Hunter, a chef in the US Army, had joined Zion's staff and was given the position I had filled for the past year and a half. This meant that Doris and I needed somewhere to live. My last day in the kitchen started early one morning when some students and staff got the idea that I was not going; that I was rebelling – I have no idea where that came from. They had me on my knees in the kitchen and were giving messages sounding like rebukes, etc. Doris was not there at the time. I do not remember how long it went on, but my recollection would suggest at least an hour. This was all part of a learning experience on this *Drive of Faith*.

Dr. Leonard Hero's mother, a great prayer warrior and woman of the Spirit, came on the scene. She looked over the situation and suddenly began to jerk her head and speak with tongues in her cute little way. Suddenly prophetic words poured forth from her mouth as she took me by the arm and marched me around the kitchen tables from one end of the kitchen to the other. The message she gave negated all the other rebukes. I do not remember all the words she used, but it was a lengthy prophetic message expressing God's appreciation for my labor of love. I do remember the last words as she quoted from an Old Testament prophet stating that when I went forth I would go with great joy and dancing; at which time she danced around the kitchen. How it all ended, I do not remember; it remains a blur in my mind. The whole experience helped me many times in this *Drive of Faith* when I was forced to let staff members go at FST for various reasons.

Our good friend who had purchased the Huppmobile for us came to our rescue. His brother, John Messerlian, was a member of Zion's church and had a nice home in Providence. John owned a grocery store and offered me a job and a place to live. Doris kept the house, prepared meals, while I delivered groceries with John's car and helped in his street corner grocery.

I had not yet started working in the store and was home with Doris helping with the cooking. John's sister, Ann, lived in the home; she was a fine Christian young lady probably in her late 20s or early 30s. She worked at a job during the day. The cooking was for four of us and on this particular day John had left us some lamb chops to broil for supper. The kitchen stove was heated by gas and the broiler was up over the cooking area at eye level. We had everything else cooking and the time was nearing for John and Ann to show up from their work. I heated the broiler up without checking the grease tray under the meat rack. We placed the Lamb chops on the meat rack and they were ready to go into the broiler. When I opened the door of the broiler, the grease in the under pan had heated to such a degree the oxygen from the open door caused it to burst into flames.

Both Doris and I jumped into action; she opened the doors next to the stove into the entry way and outside, while I reached into the broiler with a pair of cloth hot holders and brought the flaming pan of fire into the kitchen and headed toward the open door. The pan became too hot to handle and the sink was nearby, so I dumped the pan of flaming grease into the sink and quickly, without thinking, I turned on the water faucet. Within two seconds the pull shade and polka dot curtains disappeared while flames licked the sides of the cupboards.

I turned to call the fire department when suddenly the Holy Spirit came upon Doris and she pointed at the fire shouting, *In the Name of Jesus.* It would be hard to believe this if I had not seen it with my own eyes; instantly every inch of that fire disappeared down the sink drain and was gone. We began to shout praises to the God who never fails while we opened doors and windows to dissipate the smoke. That experience has helped us believe God in impossible situations many, many, times on this *Drive of Faith.* To our amazement, John and Ann had no reprimand for us; they both knew that Ann had left the grease in the pan; in fact, they were rather delighted as they got enough insurance money out of the deal to renovate the whole house.

While living with John and Ann Messerlian, I went with him to his corner grocery store every day and helped in any way I could. He asked me to drive his car and deliver groceries to some aged or handicapped that needed help. I often stocked shelves in the store with canned goods or waited on customers. I became personally acquainted with the price of food which I feel helped me in the *Drive of Faith* when I started our college.

Some interesting things happened while working in the store, one of which involved Bro. Messerlian's hired clerk. Louie was a good and trusted worker but was not able to read. One noon, when neither the owner nor I were present, a mentally handicapped man came to the store with a note for groceries. He gave the note to Louie but Louie could not read it. Louie asked the man what it said and the man told Louie to read it. A heated argument started that was about to explode, each accusing the other of being stupid. At this point Bro. Messerlian walked in, quieted them down and took the note. He read, *one loaf of bread.* Smiling, he handed the handicapped a loaf of bread and sent him on his way. I don't remember what he told Louie to do, but we should remind ourselves, *but for the grace of God, there go I.* Such things as this have helped me in this *Drive of Faith* to care more about others who were less fortunate and to appreciate the education I received at Zion Bible Institute without cost to me.

One day, just after the store cat had given birth to kittens in the back room, a man came in to buy groceries with his large German Shepherd by his side. Bro. Messerlian spoke to him quickly and asked him to take his dog outside as there was no telling what would happen if the mother cat saw a potential danger for her new family of kittens. The man would not listen and started to comment on his dog's ability to take care of any situation that might arise. About that time mother cat came strolling around the corner from the back room where her kittens were napping. When she saw Mr. Shepherd, she made one leap landing on the back of his neck and started tearing at his eyes and face. The dog high-tailed it out the door and down the street. His owner was embarrassed to say the least. That little incident helped me in this *Drive of Faith* to remember when dealing with the parents of a student: mothers are very protective of their offspring and need to be dealt with very carefully.

Chapter 29

Our First Evangelistic Services

There came a time in the middle of March, 1946, that Doris and I both felt to fast and pray about a change that was coming. I decided to tell Bro. Messerlian that the next week would be my last at the store and that sometime soon we would be moving even though we had no idea where or exactly when.

We did not want to sponge on the Messerlians if I was not helping at the store, so we sold our Huppmobile for $90 and lived off from the money we received. We had been fasting and praying about two weeks when our friend at Zion, Bro. Swan Messerlian, came to us with an offer. Pastor Goode Foster in Monticello, Maine, had asked him to come for a two week revival. Bro. Swan could not possibly go and wanted to offer our names. I felt it was an answer to our prayers and immediately agreed to go.

However, Doris wanted nothing to do with Maine. We had been to Mars Hill for a convention a few months previous and her impression of Maine was not the best. She grew up 25 miles from New York City and Maine looked too countrified for her. She had seen the houses with bales of hay around the cellar walls to keep out the cold, the big barns connected to the houses by a shed, cows in the fields, acres and acres of ground where potatoes grew, and other things that turned her off. I do not remember our conversation at the time, but I made the trip by myself.

The pastor met me at the train station and took me to a large house in the middle of Main Street. Pastor Foster and his wife, Kathryn, lived upstairs over his mother. After greetings with the family, I was shown to a large bedroom in their apartment. Meetings started sometime in the middle of

April, 1946. So here I am, all by myself, can't sing and my sermons were not more than 15 or 20 minutes long. And yet, each night God showed up; the blessing fell while Pastor played the piano and led the singing. Brother Jones would arrive a bit late during the singing, take his hat off when he came through the door, dance down the aisle to hang up his hat on the rack in the front and take a seat on the front row after the singing stopped. Brother Shaw, a one-eyed Irishman, would testify:

> *Brothers and sisters, I had a dream last night. I saw an apple orchard with huge trees but crooked rows and there wasn't an apple on any of the trees. The scene changed and I saw another orchard. The trees were small but the rows were just as straight as a die. And those trees were just loaded with apples causing the limbs to almost break.*

Nobody had to interpret his dream; it was plain. Each service ended with people getting saved or filled with the Spirit.

When Friday of that first week in Monticello rolled around, Doris had changed her mind and decided she wanted to join me. I do not know how we got in touch with each other as we had no phones. Perhaps Pastor Foster allowed me to call the Messerlians where she was staying in our room. In any case, she was on the train bound for Aroostook County, Maine, on Saturday morning. The valuable lesson I learned in this *Drive of Faith; you may sometimes have to obey God in spite of what your spouse does.* That is extremely difficult at times. Decades later I was faced with a decision of that nature where it became almost impossible to do what I knew was the right thing to do. Time proved me to be right but the work of God suffered from the decision I was forced to make. Here it is: the Apostle Paul was hindered to do the thing he knew was right; if that happens to you, you are in good company (1 Thess. 2:18, *Wherefore we would have come unto you, even I Paul, once and again; but Satan hindered us*).

The train arrived at the Monticello terminal, a lone station a couple of miles from town. There were no lights, not even a street light, near the station. The conductor would not have left Doris off the train if the Pastor and I had not been there to meet her. It was Saturday at midnight on April 20th when she arrived in the middle of a blizzard. Snow was coming down fast and covering the roads. We made it safely back to the parsonage. Needless to say, after that long trip, Doris was not ready to rise and dress for the Sunday morning service. She got a royal welcome that Sunday evening in the service where she sang the glory down. She had a special anointing every night as she ministered in testimony and song.

During the four weeks we were there, 21 were saved and 5 were filled with the Holy Ghost and Fire. There were few vehicles at the church as most of the people walked, many from distances well over a mile. One Native American family (dad, mother, and three children under 10 years of age) walked for 3 miles, one way, to service nearly every night. We would look out of our bedroom window on the second floor and watch many as they made their way walking a half hour before service. Sister Libby (Pastor Howard Libby's mother) lived on a back road. One night while walking home from our service she heard something in the woods. When she got in her door, she looked out the window to see a black bear that had been following. She was in church the next night just the same.

The meetings continued for 4 weeks until Mother's Day, May 12th. There was standing room only on that last Sunday evening with some hanging in the windows off the front porch; every seat was filled. The pastor and church wanted us to stay for at least another week, but after serious prayer we felt it was time to return to Rhode Island. Doris had a vision while praying about staying another week. The Lord showed her a hand with 1 finger and then 3 fingers. She interpreted it to mean, I had been there 1 week before she joined me for the next 3. We were so thankful we left on time as several weeks later we heard from one of the church members that they had planned to have a business meeting that next Wednesday to vote the pastor out and vote Doris and me to be pastor instead.

All in all, our experience with Pastor Goode Foster and his wife, Katheryn, was delightful; they became very good friends. One day, during the revival, he asked me to announce in the service that evening to have a pound party for the pastor. It appears that this was a common experience in

Aroostook County when the evangelist was staying in the parsonage with the pastor. People would bring dinner items and, in particular, desserts. This would relieve the burden on both the pastor and his wife who did the cooking. I asked the pastor if we could just pray and see what God would do first before asking the people. He agreed. Two or three nights later we looked at the kitchen table and counted 13 pies. Several other items came in and both the pastor and his wife were impressed. This became a principle in our *Drive of Faith,* we always looked to God and did not advertise our needs; much like George Mueller at his orphanages in England during the 19th century. While I was pastor for 18 years in Old Orchard Beach, ME, we never allowed rummage or yard sales in the name of the church; we believed the church was there to help the community, not take from them. In the early part of the 20th century, our forefathers practiced the same teaching.

Chapter 30

Landing at Last

I t was a cool morning in the middle of May, 1946, when we boarded the train and started our journey from Monticello back to Rhode Island. The trees were beginning to bud and leaves were just peeking through when we left Maine, but vegetation was in full bloom among flower blossoms when we reached Rhode Island. It was a different world that cemented the strong desire in my wife's heart to avoid Maine whenever possible. The truth was that God had already planned on Maine as the setting for this *Drive of Faith.*

Zion gave us a room to stay in during the spring convention of 1946. I am thinking it was at that time I attended the annual meeting of the Zion Evangelistic Fellowship and we became members. It was a ministerial organization connected with the college that granted credentials to ministers actively engaged in the ministry. Doris and I developed a friendship with a McClurg missionary couple during our few days at the convention. The McClurgs invited us to travel with them to some conventions in Northern Maine during the month of June. Our journey took us through Bangor, Maine, where the differential on the shaft broke and we had to have it replaced. Doris and I stayed with a godly couple in Lincoln, ME, who operated a cleaning business (clothes). We attended the Pentecostal church where Pastor Cyrus Tarbox was the minister; I believe the McClurgs preached and shared about their ministry in China.

It took nearly a week to get the part for the McCurg's car, but finally we were on our way to the Caribou convention where Evangelist Gene Kimball was preaching and Robert Pinkham was pastor. It appears that this trip back to Maine was telling Doris something about Maine on this *Drive of*

Faith, but I am sure she was not anxious to listen. In the remainder of the trip to Maine I learned in the conventions to develop some of Billy Sunday's style in my preaching and how to feed and house people. Al of these I used later in this *Drive of Faith.*

The first night of the Caribou convention was interesting. There were about 20-30 preachers on the platform when Evangelist Kimball began to preach. He was great at using people for props in his message. He put one of my colleagues, Lloyd Sharp (later became missionary to Africa) in a closet on the side of the platform, illustrating Elijah in the cave. Bro. Kimball would open the door and peek in to ask how Elijah was doing about every 3 or 4 minutes. He had the audience in a roar of laughter. He used so many preachers that night, but on the second night they all went to seats in the audience before the preaching began. What did Evangelist Kimball do? He went down off the platform and chose a quiet preacher/teacher (from Zion Bible Institute) in the front row. He brought him up to the pulpit to read a Scripture for him. It was Job 16:12; *I was at ease, but he hath broken me asunder: he hath also taken me by my neck, and shaken me to pieces, and set me up for his mark.* While Rev. Henry Sinclair was reading, Bro. Kimball illustrated by repeating, saying, *He didn't take him by the waist and shake him* (at which moment he shook Bro. Sinclair by the waist), *he took him by the neck.* Bro. Kimball made a menacing gesture as he quickly took his hands from the waist and grabbed him by the neck. This brought a gasp from the audience as they watched intently at what was coming next.

Bro. Kimball's hands fell from the neck and he reached down and picked Bro. Sinclair up in his arms and tossed him into a seat on the platform – preaching all the time during this action. Most of the preachers stayed far away from the platform after the second night. It is easy for me to learn sports or anything else by observing. As a young preacher of 20, I learned many things from watching Evangelist Kimball preaching in his Billy Sunday style. These were a blessing to me in this *Drive of Faith.*

From Caribou we went with McClurgs to the Washburn, Maine convention. I do not remember much about the speaker or housing except that they had some mighty good cooks in that church. It was my privilege twenty or more years later to preach the Washburn convention several times. One of those times they were between pastors so that they considered me their pastor and convention speaker for the 10 days I was there. This taught me much about filling important positions all at once in this *Drive of Faith*. I have had to do that a few times.

When we returned to Rhode Island, we made plans to travel to western New York State with the McClurgs where we could catch a bus to my parent's home. Our two or three medium size suitcases held all our belongings. We found a place for them in the trunk of the McClurg's car and took our place in the rear seat. The car was pointed toward Western New York. The exact routes I do not remember, but I do know that we ended up on Route 20 between Albany and Buffalo. New York State Throughway was only a dream at that time. We must have stopped somewhere overnight as it was midafternoon when we arrived in Canandaigua, a town just south of Rochester at the head of Canandaigua Lake. We bought bus tickets to Erie, PA where my father would pick us up. After the tickets were purchased, we had only a bit of change left in our pockets. But what more did we need; God had provided to that point and we were headed to our destination. This has often been the case on this wonderful *Drive of Faith*; just enough, not too much, but we always have made it.

The trip from Erie to East Kane, PA, in my father's car has disappeared from my memory. Neither can I remember how my poor family arranged their sleeping accommodations during the few weeks Doris and I were there. All my siblings were still home; my oldest sister was 19 and my youngest brother was 7; the remainder being 17, 15, 13, 11, and 9. The experiences that came with being raised in a large family have been helpful in this *Drive of Faith;* we all learned to sacrifice, give and take a little, and get along with what we had available.

My parents' pastor was the same pastor that we had when we got saved in Westfield, NY. The whole family thought a great deal of Pastor Theodore Terry. He gave me a chance to preach and to help him in the services. During the week, he held a service in Ludlow, a small town nearby. The Larsons lived there on the property; that is where I first got acquainted with Keith who became a great pastoral friend of mine. Keith Larson became the pastor in Smithport, PA, where I had the opportunity, 3 decades later, to minister a number of times. His daughter graduated from FST in the 80's.

An interesting thing happened at one midweek service in Ludlow. It was a small group who met in a cottage waiting for Pastor Terry. He dropped me off to start the service while he made a house call on the sick. Now Pastor Terry was adamant about his interpretation of 1 Cor. 14:27; *There must never be more than 3 messages in tongues in one church service.* While I was leading the service, someone gave a message in tongues and another interpreted it before Pastor returned. After he returned, there were 3 more messages in tongues and Pastor Terry interpreted each one. He did this without knowing about the message before he arrived. I do not know if anyone ever told him, but Doris and I took particular notice as we had been taught differently in college. You may remember reading in a previous chapter in this *Drive of Faith* story that the verse limits the number of messages one person should give, and thus puts no limit on the Holy Spirit.

One of the greatest honors of the summer of '46 was the privilege Pastor Terry gave me to fill in for his pastoral duties while he and his family went on vacation. We were asked to live at the parsonage and minister in all the services until he returned. Pastor Terry wanted to get us started as pioneer pastors in Clearfield, PA. He indicated that the Assembly of God district office would contribute forty dollars ($40) weekly for one year to help us. After prayerful consideration, we declined to take the offer. We had done the same when a similar offer was made for us to pioneer in Clinton, Mass. I was chomping at the bit, anxious to get started in our life's work, but we felt we must have a personal approval from God. This has always been our stand as we rode down the *Drive of Faith* over these past many years.

The time came in August of 1946 when we had to say *good bye* to my family and make our bus ride to New Jersey. Route 6 across the top of Pennsylvania is a long trip on the bus, but eventually we arrived in Denville, New Jersey. There we met Doris' mother and rode three or four miles back to her home on Morris Avenue in Mountain Lakes. Sister Rosen (Doris' mother) was one of the finest ladies I ever knew; I was blessed to call her my mother-in-law. She was a great inspiration to me personally as I traveled on this *Drive of Faith*. What an honor the family gave me to preach her funeral service in 1999; she was 100 years old.

When we arrived I immediately looked for work as we were not sure how long we would be there. On this *Drive of Faith* we learned that sometimes we had to lower ourselves to manual labor; when you live by faith it does not mean that you sit and wait for provisions to come if you can provide some other way. I found work in a plant that manufactured fuses for the railways and the military. It was dangerous work as the powder used in the fuses could ignite and cause an explosion but it paid well so I took the job. It was within walking distance of the house.

I stayed on that job about 8 weeks until one day my wife and I felt to write our college president and ask if she knew of any place of ministry for Doris and me. This was right after my 21st birthday in October. We got a response from Sister Gibson immediately, asking me to come and talk with her. I made arrangements to board a train in the neighboring town of Boonton. A couple of connections, one of which was Grand Central in New York City, brought me to my final destination in Providence, RI. I grabbed a streetcar which took me to six corners in East Providence, just a couple of blocks from 846 Broadway and Zion Bible Institute. Sister Gibson called me in and chatted with me right after supper. She looked at me and said, *Brother Pier, the only thing I can think of when I pray is Old Orchard Beach, Maine.* She explained the ins and outs of the situation; mainly how so many had attempted to start a Pentecostal church there and had to give up. I listened intently and then went to call my wife in New Jersey.

Relief and a little surprised was I when Doris responded with, "*I knew it all the time!*" She felt the Lord had spoken to her while I was in Rhode Island and indicated it would be Old Orchard Beach, Maine. So after a year of telling the Lord she wanted any place but Maine, she was about to spend the next 55 happy years of her life and be buried in a cemetery at Corinth, Maine.

When I got back to New Jersey the next day, we packed up and bought train tickets from Penn Station in Newark to Grand Central in NYC. Mother transported us from home to Newark and stayed with us until we boarded the train. Both Doris and I knew we did not have enough money to buy tickets from Grand Central to Providence, but neither of us breathed a word to anyone. In 1946 the tickets from NYC to Rhode Island were four dollars and twenty six cents each ($4.26). I had exactly six dollars ($6.00) in my pocket. We had put our trust in God, and if He was in this, He would provide. That is paramount in this *Drive of Faith;* let God talk to people so He gets the glory.

The train was pulling in at the underground platform at Penn Station. We picked up our suitcases and started for the steps leading into the Pullman. While others were boarding ahead of us, mother grabbed my sleeve and said in quick tones, *"How much money do you have?"* I quickly shook my head for her not to worry while I picked up the suitcase I had dropped when she took hold of my sleeve. Insistently she demanded that I tell her. Finally I said, *"I have $6 in my wallet".* She said, *"Give me that",* while she quickly took a $10 bill from her purse, grabbed my six and pushed the $10 into my hand. This all happened within seconds as I picked up the suitcase again. We managed to get on the train just as the conductor was calling out, *"All aboard!"* This was another God-given test on this *Drive of Faith.*

After a streetcar ride from the train station in Providence to Six Corners, we walked about 2 city blocks to Zion. After settling in a room for the night, we contacted our good friends, Bill and Amy Springer. They were junior students in their 30s and hailed from Lincoln, Maine. They agreed to transport us the next day, October 26, 1946, to Old Orchard Beach.

Old Orchard Street, Old Orchard Beach in 1940s

Chapter 31

Old Orchard Beach, Here We Come

It was Saturday morning when we left for our journey into a State where I would spend the next 60 years preaching the Gospel. It was a trip of about 140 miles through cities and towns as there were no Interstate roads at that time. Bill and Amy Springer were friends we needed on this *Drive of Faith;* friends are important on any *drive of faith.*

Sometime that afternoon we pulled up to some high steps leading to the door of 76 Washington Avenue in Old Orchard Beach. We had been given the keys and told which door they would open at Zion's *cottage.* What a surprise – cottage? It was a nine room, 3 story house, situated on a ridge beside several other large homes. We opened the door with wonder in our eyes. The first floor was well furnished and boasted beautiful hardwood floors. It was a cool day so Brother Springer helped me start the oil burner in the kitchen stove.

Later we would discover that there was a coal-fired steam boiler in the cellar that would heat the whole house. The catch, however, was it cost money, lots of it, to have coal delivered and with just my wife and me, we did not need heat in nine rooms. All of those facts were quite a test of faith and wisdom. We learned on this *Drive of Faith* that God's money was to be spent wisely and not wasted. Heat, food, and a roof overhead were 3 essentials to stay alive in the State of Maine.

Before Bill and Amy left, we opened the door to a small pantry closet in the kitchen. There was a can of baked beans and outside of a few cleaning products, that was what stood between us and going hungry. Bill and Amy had prayer with us and bid us farewell. I must have been given a few dollars when I was at Zion those few hours, but I do not remember. Where we went to church that next day, I do not remember; there were 3 protestant churches, all within walking distance of our address. The Salvation Army was closest, and the Methodist was a few blocks down our street. I am not sure if the Advent Christian Church was open at that time.

We managed to survive the weekend. On Monday evening we were both surprised and blessed to have a visit from Sister Gibson. She had some staff from Zion with her and was traveling back to Rhode Island from the convention in Mars Hill, Maine. The farmers in Mars Hill and the surrounding towns provided a rail car full of potatoes for Zion's tables. It was customary for Sister Gibson to attend the convention and show her appreciation for their gift. She stayed only a few minutes before placing a $20 bill in my hand. Her parting words to me were, *"Brother Pier, I leave you to the mercy of God!"* What better place to put us but in bed with God's grace and mercy. A *Drive of Faith* needs lots of both.

During the month of November, we had postcard size announcements made and walked the streets (we had no vehicle) of Old Orchard Beach and invited everyone we could to the first service. That effort brought us in contact with several interesting individuals. The Shoreys lived next door to us. Sister Shorey (they were believers from the Salvation Army Chapel) said, *"You will never have a Pentecostal church here; those two ladies with lots of talent tried so hard and they had to quit"*. I called on Charles and Nettie Trafton, Evergreen Ave., precious Pentecostal saints. Nettie's sister was the pastor at the Landing Chapel in Kennebunk. Traftons were a retired couple in their 70s. Sister Nettie put her fist down lightly on the small table in her parlor and said, *"Brother Pier, you will never have a Pentecostal church in this town"*. Within a year, Nettie became one of our most ardent supporters; you better not say anything derogatory about Brother Pier to Nettie Trafton. Seriously, I love those words telling me it would never be when I knew what God had said. That experience has been repeated several times on this *Drive of Faith*.

One more call at 29 Ocean Avenue was extremely interesting. Pastor Robert and Amy Wallace, ministers at the Assembly of God in Portland (about 15 miles from Old Orchard Beach), welcomed us in their home. Pastor Wallace was a presbyter and well known in the area as a holiness preacher. His high school daughter was the piano player in his church, but when he found out she walked home from school with an unsaved male, he removed her from the piano bench. He told me two things I have never forgotten; 1) *I will never help you but I won't hurt you,* and 2) *there is a curse on that building up there (our chapel) and you will never have a Pentecostal church there.* He explained as to why he thought there was a curse which I am not going to reiterate as it would take too much room here and would not be edifying. I learned on this *Drive of Faith* to expect most anything and then just shout the victory as the blessing comes marching around the corner.

Pastor Bob Wallace ended up helping me several times; he shared eggs, bacon, and other foods that farmers in his church gave him. On top of that, he had me pick a new year's calendar (1947) when I called on him the first part of January. He explained that on New Year's Eve he and his wife prayed over these calendars and gave each member one for their home. With each calendar was a promise and he told me how many times the promises had spoken to different members who chose them. He had about a dozen left over; passed me the basket and had me choose one. I did so and he asked that I read the promise that came with the one I chose. His face blushed somewhat when I read these words from Deuteronomy: *but the LORD thy God turned the curse into a blessing unto thee, because the LORD thy God loved thee.* I have forgotten what he said after that, but I shall never forget how I felt when I walked up the street to the little Zion Gospel Chapel at 100 Ocean Avenue. These challenges were so very important at the beginning of our ministry in Old Orchard Beach; necessary challenges on this *Drive of Faith.*

We bought two 1x12" boards, fourteen and twelve feet long. We painted them white and printed large black letters spelling *Zion Gospel Chapel.* I asked the Lord for directions as to how I could nail these to the front of the chapel about 12 or 14 feet above the ground. I had a ladder, the nails, and a hammer; but how was I going to do this alone? He put the idea in my head and this is how I did it. I took a rope, tied loop in it about the size of the board, climbed the ladder to the height I wanted the sign, and nailed a spike that would hold the loop. I took the newly painted board, climbed the ladder that I placed in the middle of the building just above the steps, put one end of the board in the loop at the end of the building, and fastened the end I held with one nail. Placed the ladder over by the loop, made sure sign was straight with the clapboards, and fastened it securely with nails. I reckon you can picture the rest of the story about the other part of the sign, but when I finished, one man had installed a good looking sign, and he was feeling pleased.

It was Sunday, December 8, 1946, when Zion Gospel Chapel, 100 Ocean Avenue, Old Orchard Beach, Maine, opened its doors that still remain open after 73 years. It is now located at 47 Smithwheel Road as Faith Lighthouse. This is the church that was told it would never be. All of its doubters lay waiting for the resurrection while the Drive of Faith moves on.

The first service was scheduled for 3 PM. About noon that day I went to the chapel to start a fire. A one register furnace, located in the cellar, had not seen a fire for about 4 or 5 years. Dampness had settled in which caused the furnace to smoke. I opened the front door and what windows I could. Just at that moment, John Connors, the Methodist church janitor was walking by on his way home from church. I breathed a sigh of relief when he offered to help me. He explained to this green horn pastor why it was smoking. It was then that I realized I should have tried starting this furnace the day before, to get it cleared out after sitting unused for so long. The air in the chapel eventually cleared and the service started on time. Another lesson on this Drive of Faith; when you do what God has asked, He always has someone there to help in time of need.

Seven souls sat waiting to be fed from God's Word at 3 PM. Among them were Bro. and Sis. Charles Trafton, Sis. Mable Elliott, and Sis. Connors. I preached from a text taken from the Book of Proverbs; *Remove not the ancient landmark, which thy fathers have set.* No one made a commitment that day, but it was a beginning. I had heard that leaders in the past had talked a lot about money, so I determined for the first few years I would take no offering. I left a basket at the table beside the door and mentioned the same when I gave the announcements. Usually there was a dollar or two; occasionally there would be five dollars and we felt a revival was near at hand. In this *Drive of Faith*, the less said about money was best. We never broadcasted our needs; God got all the glory for answered prayer.

Thursday evening we had prayer and Bible study. Many times there was no one present. When that happened, Doris and I would don our aprons, get out the paint cans and brushes, and work. There was always someone present on Sunday, but a few times I preached to as few as three people. John Connors, the brother mentioned above that helped me with the fire, took me aside one day. These were his words as I remember them; *"Rev., if you could just leave those "tongues" out, you could fill that chapel; you are the best preacher in town"*. I should have told him what one preacher said under similar circumstances; *"Sir, if we didn't have what you don't like, we wouldn't have what you do like"*.

The winter of '46-'47 was brutal and we did not have enough money to keep coal in the cellar. We kept the oil fire going in the kitchen stove on the first floor and slept in a cold, cold bedroom upstairs. I left the water running in the bathtub in the second floor bathroom; ice built up some 6 inches thick in the bottom but the line never froze. I went downstairs to the kitchen one morning to find the thermometer reading 32 and the oil fire was still on. We turned up the oil and made it through the day and the months to the next fall. There have been lots of such difficulties in this *Drive of Faith*, but victory came as we persisted and stayed with the ship.

74 Washington Avenue

Chapter 32

Pioneering Two Churches

Easter Sunday, April 6, 1947, in Old Orchard Beach is a date I will always remember. About 10 people were the most we had in any service since opening day. When I looked down at the crowd of 20 in Zion Gospel Chapel that afternoon, I thought surely revival had come. Doris did a great job on the piano during song service and later sang a beautiful solo. I do not remember my text but I shall never forget the thrill that came over me from head to feet when I saw 3 adults and 2 teenagers coming to the altar for salvation. This was a thrilling event on the *Drive of Faith* which gave us the assurance that rewards do come to those who remain faithful in their work for Jehovah.

Mable Elliott, a woman near 50, surrendered her heart to God that day and served Him the rest of her life. If my memory serves me right, she was the mother of 4 girls and 1 boy. All five were eventually saved at our altars. Two of her children graduated from Zion Bible College in the next decade and worked in the ministry their entire lives. Her oldest daughter and husband became some of our closest friends in the Old Orchard Beach church. Her daughter taught Sunday School for years and her son in law served on our board as church treasurer. Her youngest daughter, Kay, married Jesse Owen and is still serving in missionary evangelistic work. Kay was the first person I baptized in water. One of the blessings on this *Drive of Faith* is knowing that the *gift goes on – it keeps giving, and giving, and giving again.*

It would take too long to tell the whole story about that family; suffice it to say, Mable, her oldest daughter, Arlene and her husband Bob, Mable's youngest daughter, Kathrine, were 4 of the 5 saved that Easter Sunday of

1947 and every single one of them remained true to the Lord all their lives. They all became pillars in our church for many years. Kathrine, Arlene, and Bob were the first I ever baptized in water. The event took place in the summer of 1947, in Milliken Pond on Portland Avenue, Old Orchard Beach.

One more incident should be mentioned that took place in the spring of 1947. Our faith was being tested when for three days we had little to eat except carrots and potatoes. We raw fried them one day, boiled them the next day, and creamed them the last day. But what a day of rejoicing at the end of that test when several boxes arrived that we did not know were coming from the youth group in the Rockaway, NJ, Assembly of God (Doris' home church). We had no vehicle so I walked the mile to the station and carried the boxes on my shoulder, one by one. It took several trips. We piled the groceries on the kitchen table, stacking them a couple of feet high, and stood rejoicing and praising God for our kind friends in Rockaway. I had the opportunity to preach in that church dozens of times over the years, and thanked them over and over for their kindness. Wow, we could hardly find room in our small pantry for all those goodies. Beloved, this incident had a lasting effect on our faith over the years as we traveled on this *Drive of Faith*.

From October, 1946, to June of 1947, we traveled by shoe leather express or local buses that originated in Biddeford about five miles away. One of our requests in daily prayers was for a vehicle. It was a mighty surprise when we discovered the way God answered that prayer. A maiden lady, a solid Nazarene Christian, in her seventies, began attending our services. She saw the difficulty we were having with no transportation. One Sunday she approached me and laid out an offer that seemed too good to be true.

She had a home situated a little over a mile on the other side of town. A relative of hers drove the car she owned to transport her to places she needed to go. The plan she gave me went like this:

I go to work five days a week at seven in the morning at the shoe factory in Biddeford (approximately seven miles from her home). I finish work at four in the afternoon. If you will drive me to and from my work each day, you may use my car as your own for church related functions, travel to regional church services, go shopping or for whatever need you have.

Now you know why the offer of that little old lady seemed too good to be true. Miss Edith Blades became a close friend of ours during our ministry at Old Orchard Beach. Doris and I drove her home in the car she let us use, and the next morning I was on time, at about 6:30, sitting outside her farmhouse door on Portland Avenue. The car had been parked in my driveway all night. I made the trip, morning and afternoon, every day month after month.

Do you have any idea what this car meant to a young, twenty one year old preacher, in 1946? It was a new, beautiful black, shiny, '46 fluid drive Dodge, four-door; the envy of any minister in those days. I did not have to pay for the registration, insurance, nor upkeep; it was mine to use for the Lord's work. This experience on the *Drive of Faith* helped us see God working in various ways to answer prayer and bring about His purpose in our lives.

For some reason, Miss Edith Blades felt to sell the Dodge and give me one thousand dollars to go to New Jersey and buy a brand new 1947 Kaiser for myself. It is unclear in my mind at this date, but it seems that the shoe factory either closed down or Miss Blades felt to quit her job. At any rate, Doris and I made the trip to New Jersey, bought the Kaiser, and signed for the payments. The details of the deal are very turbid, clouded with unsettled factors to which Doris and I were not accustomed. We never signed for debts unless we had good reason to know how we would make the payments. This has been a practice of mine on this *Drive of Faith*.

The end results of the Kaiser deal was another trip to New Jersey within the next twelve months to swap cars with my father-in-law. He took over the payments and gave us his 1936 Plymouth. I will never forget the euphoria that filled our hearts as Doris and I drove back to Maine in a stick shift, medium blue Plymouth, praising God for relief from that debt. Another payment situation at that time sealed our commitment to pay cash or a very small payment within our budget, and only one payment at a time. In other words, we learned to buy the washing machine and not try to get anything else until that was completely paid. We learned early on this *Drive of Faith* that debt can destroy a marriage, and it was to be avoided whenever possible.

Our weekly free add about our church in the Biddeford newspaper attracted one of the finest families that ever darkened our church door. Kenneth and Dorothy Taylor of Arundel, Maine, made the twelve mile journey to 100 Ocean Avenue in Old Orchard Beach for our Sunday afternoon service. Kenneth was the manager of a feed company supplying the farmers of the area with grain and supplements for their industry. They lived on a small farm where they had their own milk cow, chickens, etc. They blessed Doris and me multiple times with eggs, chickens, and food that became an answer to prayers. We sat at the Taylor's dining room table and enjoyed some of the best country cooking anywhere. At one of those times, Brother Taylor told me of a country church in the area that had not had services of any kind for at least twenty years. It was located about two miles from his home on a dirt road. He was personally acquainted with some elderly people who had authority over the property.

Sometime in the late 1920s the North Chapel on the Limerick Road in Arundel, Maine, closed its doors for the last time before Brother Taylor and I paid it a visit in 1948. We arranged for a legal North Chapel business meeting with a half a dozen elderly saints whose names were still on the roll. They voted to allow us the opportunity to take charge of the property and open the church for services.

The building, built in 1850, was in serious need of repair. The floor had waves like the sea and plaster was falling off the ceiling. I stood at the large pulpit and peeked through the ceiling and roof above at the blue sky. A stove pipe ran the distance in the auditorium from the back of the church to the attic chimney just above the pulpit. 32 small panes of glass were broken, and many shingles were missing from the roof. I had the privilege to show the project to several preachers and nearly every one of them told me it could never be done and that I was foolish to try. My adrenaline springs alive when auricle picks up such challenges; the *Drive of Faith* has seen dozens of these over the years.

There are a lot of wonderful stories I could tell you about North Chapel. Fortunately I had a group of young people that helped us and some of the men assisted for the heavy items such as jacking up the floor; and shingling the roof. There was no electric and in those days no Pentecostal would have ever thought of having church without a Sunday evening service for his family. I cannot think of any better place to be with family on a Lord's Day evening than with jubilant saints as they listen to an evangelistic message and watch sinners kneeling at the altar. So I bought an electrician's book and wired the building by myself. I hired an electrician to check it over and connect it to the newly installed meter. North Chapel had service every Sunday evening while I was pastor.

During the four years that I was the pastor, we saw many saved, baptized in water, filled with the Holy Spirit, and healed in that old country church on a dirt road. Supernatural things happened such as angels appearing which those in attendance witnessed. One middle-aged Christian Advent lady was shook up one evening while I was preaching. She had heard about an angel appearing when I was preaching but she had doubts. Suddenly it appeared by my side (I never saw it) and she said right out loud, *Oh, there it is!* She grabbed her mouth, embarrassed. This sister was very meticulous about her appearance. One evening she was seated on the front pew during the altar service where saints were receiving the Holy Ghost. Suddenly the Holy Spirit hit her and she plopped squarely down on the floor where her feet had been. I watched as she quickly grabbed her hat to straighten it and picked herself up off the floor. She was visibly shaken; she had never experienced anything like that before.

It was at that service that one of our new converts, a Native American lady, lay prostrate on the floor seeking the outpouring of the Holy Spirit. Her expression would have troubled some people, but it was her simple plea to be filled with the Spirit. *Come on in, old boy, come on in,* was her cry. Those who heard her were bug eyed and I am sure they wondered if I was going to stop her, when all of a sudden she began to speak in a beautiful tongue of a language she did not know. Evidently the Holy Spirit did not mind the words she used; it was one of her customary simple verbal expressions.

North Chapel was an exciting part of my life for the next four years. Doris and I taught Sunday School in the morning at that old country church on a dirt road (about 12 miles from Old Orchard Beach), and ministered at the morning service; her at the piano and me preaching. We left church somewhere near 12:30, stopped in Biddeford for a bite to eat, and landed in Old Orchard Beach for Sunday School at 2:00. The afternoon service in Old Orchard Beach began at 3:00 and I was the pastor and preacher. I left alone about 6:15 to reach the Old North Chapel by 7:00 to start the service and preach. Doris started the service in Zion Gospel Chapel, Old Orchard Beach, at 7:45. She led the singing, prayer, and testimonies (in those days most Pentecostal churches had testimonies). I left Old North Chapel at 8:15 to race through two cities (Biddeford and Saco) and walk into the service at 8:45 in time to preach. Hallelujah, the *Drive of Faith* never knew a dull moment.

It was my pleasure to preach four times every Sunday for four years and never be exhausted or weary. I take no credit for that. God blessed me with an extra pocket of energy; all the glory goes to Him. I was seldom ever sick; in fact, I really do not remember ever being sick enough to miss a preaching service in those four years. Please do not pin any roses on me; Jesus did it all; He just happened to choose me for His vessel at that time. The *Drive of Faith* has been filled with times like this; it would be easy to fill several pages with testimonies of His amazing grace that made it possible.

The 1946 Dodge

Chapter 33

The Next Four Unforgettable Years

During my fourth year at North Chapel I was tapped by Rev. Christine Gibson, president of Zion Bible Institute (my Alma Mater), to teach in the college at East Providence, RI. I provided candidates to pastor North Chapel and they chose Rev. Howard Libby. Teaching in Rhode Island involved a hundred and forty mile one way trip every week. I taught class on Tuesday afternoon and Wednesday morning, usually spoke in the 11 AM chapel service Wednesday and often was asked by the pastor of Zion Temple, Rev. Leonard Heroo, to preach at the Wednesday evening service. This was a tremendous learning experience that assisted me along on this *Drive of Faith.*

Prophecy, Dispensational Truth, and Doctrine 2 (Angelology, Sanctification, Pneumatology), were the courses assigned to me. It was thrilling and mentally challenging to prepare lessons every week for both the Junior and Senior classes. Sister Gibson saw to it that I was given ten dollars every week to cover gas expense. Gas was twenty one cents a gallon in those days, so the ten dollars covered more than just fuel. Occasionally some individual at the college felt the urge of the Spirit to give me a gift that helped with car payments, etc. Rodney Drake from Bucksport, ME, was a student at that time; he handed me a twenty dollar bill. I have never forgotten that experience as it was such an answer to prayer. Rodney was standing with Norene Center who later became his wife, when he handed me that gift outside on the campus. In this *Drive of Faith* I have forgotten the names of hundreds who gave hundreds, but it was often the small blessings like that of Rodney's that met a special need that was hard to forget.

One Wednesday evening in Zion Gospel Temple I stood to read my text from Luke 5:26; *And they were all amazed, and they glorified God, and were filled with fear, saying, We have seen strange things to day.* Before I said another word (just as if it had been planned), a rock as large as a big fist came through the top of a stained glass window landing in the middle of the aisle some twenty plus feet from the wall. Not one piece of glass or debris touched the people under the path of that rock. The whole church was in awe when they realized what had happened; truly, we had seen a strange thing as God protected His people that night. Such supernatural protection and provision has taken place numerous times during this *Drive of Faith*.

Here are two events during my time of teaching at Zion that shall never be forgotten. I have substituted names in both of these stories for obvious reasons. The first event happened in a daily chapel service where I was asked to speak. During the message I stopped in my train of thought to tell some young man these words. *There is a male student here this morning who has been ostracized by some because of untrue gossip suggesting he is a homosexual. God wants him to know that He has seen his tears and heard his cry. Lift up your head, my brother, and continue your walk with God. He will vindicate you and bless your efforts to follow His call.*

At the close of the service, a young man met me at the front with tears streaming down his face. He babbled out some thanks while wiping the water away and told me his story. He went on to serve the Lord and later on, relatives of his attended FST. That was such an important event that has helped me multiple times during this *Drive of Faith*. Unsubstantiated stories can ruin lives; it is important to hear all the facts.

The last story I will relate about my years of teaching in Zion happened at a graduation banquet. The banquet was held in the college dining hall. Decorations were beautifully displayed and the seating arranged in orderly fashion. During the program each senior gave a testimony. I do not remember any of the testimonies, nor do I remember even one word in the remarks made by this senior. The names are fictitious for obvious reasons.

There was no apparent reason for me to react in the Holy Spirit as I did; Felicia was not emotional, just simply giving her testimony like her classmates. All of a sudden there arose within me a horrible weeping and groaning. I tried for a moment to suppress it until I was sure it was coming from the Spirit of God. Just as she ended her words, I broke out groaning in the Spirit. I had to kneel at an empty chair nearby and started weeping with continued groaning. Finally, speaking in tongues I uttered a message in between those emotional groans and got up and quietly took my seat.

They waited; no interpretation. The program continued and nothing more was said. The next morning my heart was concerned about Felicia; I knew her family well. In fact, her family was well known in her State as singers and had been in Pentecost a long time. Felicia herself was a talented young lady. After breakfast, with Felicia heavy on my heart, I left the dining hall for my room in the Grace More building. Outside steps led to the second floor hall and my room was the first on the left. Going up the steps, I was praying, asking God to send Felicia to me if I was to talk to her about last night. When I opened the door at the top of the stairs, who was coming down the hall with her Bible under her arm but Felicia. *"Brother Pier, I need to see you"*, were her words spoken when she was yet 25 feet away. I invited her in, sat her down next to the open door, and I took a seat by the window some ten feet away.

She began to unload something like this; Brother Pier, you know that Doug and I have been going together for some time and have been planning our wedding next month. Several of the staff here at Zion have talked with me about this and tried to discourage us. Many have been against our friendship. I have been praying this week that God would show you if this wasn't right. (well thank you, Felicia – went through my brain) Then that happened last night at the banquet. I went to Brother Hagerman and asked if he got anything from your demonstration. (Bro. Hagerman was a trusted professor at the college, one that I had a lot of respect for; he was used more than any other staff member for interpretations). He assured me that last night's spiritual demonstration was God's blessing on plans for marriage.

Felicia continued; I want God's will but I have had some doubts. So many of the staff who live here on campus have been against us, and that is the reason I asked God to show you. You are here only a couple days a week and I believe you are a man of God I can trust. Tell me the truth, Brother Pier, what do you think God was saying last night?

My response; "I don't know what He was saying, but I am sure He is not pleased with something and the Holy Spirit was praying for the situation. Those groans I felt and tears that came were not God's approval. It would be wrong for me to tell you the will of God for your life; that is something you need to hear from His lips. My advice is that you take plenty of time and seek His face earnestly. You and Doug have your whole lives and ministries before you; to find the center of God's will and do it will make the difference when you stand before Him when it is all over".

We continued to talk for a few more minutes and then I offered to pray for her and the decision she had to make. She left on good terms and I assured her of continued prayer from my heart. This talk was within a day or two of her graduation. Felicia left Zion, returned to her home and planned her marriage during the latter part of June.

Working in my office in the basement church at Old Orchard Beach, I received a message (not sure, at this time if it was via phone or mail) that Felicia and Doug were to be married the following Friday. It was Tuesday when the message came, and with it a word from heaven to my soul. The Holy Spirit fervently prompted me to write Felicia at once and warn her not to proceed with that marriage. I obeyed; sat at the typewriter and carefully chose the proper words to express what the Spirit was telling me.

The letter was sent in a sealed envelope within another envelope addressed to her pastor with a note. I remember clearly that it was sent on Tuesday and the pastor received it on Thursday, the day before the wedding. Her pastor was a colleague of mine and I trusted him to give the sealed envelope to Felicia when no one was around; I wanted no one to interfere with what God was saying to her while she read it. She read it carefully and would have called the wedding off if....

Yes, this will be hard for you to believe, but I am relating it with a clear mind, remembering each detail. This came from Felicia's mouth and was confirmed by her pastor. I knew nothing of these facts before I wrote the letter. Felicia and Doug were asked to sing and say something at the Sunday morning service prior to my letter and their wedding. At the end of their song a respected sister in the audience, one who often gave messages, got up from her seat speaking in tongues and stood behind Felicia and Doug by the pulpit. The interpretation was given by a respected visiting preacher stating the blessing of God on their coming union. It was later reported that the lady who gave the message felt like she had just done an awful thing when she took her seat, but she never told that until weeks later.

If that had not happened, Felicia would have broken with Doug when she received my letter and the next day wedding would not have taken place. Four weeks from the day that I wrote the letter, Felicia and her mother were sitting in my church office in Old Orchard Beach, tearfully relating the rest of this story.

The details of our conversation are cloudy since this took place over sixty years ago; however, I do recall the tears and sobs coming from Felicia as she unfolded the events of the previous four weeks. The wedded couple and all their belongings had arrived at an apartment in the large city. Among Doug's luggage was a medium sized trunk that Felicia had not seen. At some time or other within the first week, Felicia had the chance to paw through the contents of that trunk and discovered Doug had lied to her about his family. Much of her findings are confidential that I do not feel right to share, but the marriage received a serious blow, or you might say an explosion. It was all over from the start. Felicia had reason to fear for her life. And here she was in my office pouring out her soul to the one she asked God to show her His will.

Her mother said very little other than to comfort this talented daughter that had made a terrible mistake. Mother did have something to say, however, when I counseled Felicia about her future. She had signed the contract that was declared by her pastor (and God's Word) to be *until death do us part*. I remember mother's words as though they were uttered yesterday; *Oh, you can't do that, Brother Pier, she is just a young woman!* Romans chapter seven had suddenly been ripped from mother's Bible; *For the woman which hath an husband is bound by the law to her husband so long as he liveth; ...So then if, while her husband liveth, she be married to another man, she shall be called an adulteress.*

When I reminisce on the advice I gave her, I regret that I did not know the details of the marriage laws. I feel certain now that Felicia had every right, both legally and Scripturally to have her marriage properly annulled. Any contract based on a lie can be broken. Today I would tell any believer that God does not expect you to live under a contract that was based on a falsehood. I know of at least one other young person that I would have advised (if I had been asked) to do the same thing; she was told on her wedding night in the motel that he never really loved her; he only married her because ...! Marriage is a serious life-long partnership that should never begin with an untruth.

Felicia and I have never crossed paths from that day to this and it has been sixty or more years. Anything I have heard about her is only rumor and would not be proper to print here. I would advise any of my readers to know God for yourself; listen to a man or woman of God who gives you warning, but in the end obey what you know personally as the will of God.

The four years I taught at Zion were valuable in preparing me for my life's work as the founder and president of Faith School of Theology. I was elected as the alumni president of Zion in 1956 and served until I left the college in 1958.

I had studied diligently previous to teaching and earned a Bachelor of Arts degree in Bible from the American Divinity College, Chicago, ILL. I still do not know why I took up studying for a degree except that I had an insatiable urge for knowledge.

One of the courses I took was Public Speaking. I had no idea that several years later I would write my own course in Public Speaking that would become one of the hallmarks of my teaching. The first class I taught in Public Speaking was in 1959 when FST originated and they are still teaching from my textbook today. Hundreds of preachers are using what they learned in those classes throughout these many years. It goes to show you that God ordains things in your life along the way to prepare you for places of ministry down the road. I have to say that this happened many, many times during this *Drive of Faith.*

Here is a small insert that I think my readers will enjoy. In the mid 1990s I had the opportunity to teach my course in Public Speaking to 32 Russians who sat in my class in Breast, Belarus. On the day of the practice of their master speech, they did terrible. I spoke to the class to prepare them for the next day when they would do it for the last time and it would affect their final grade. My simple message was, *I thought that you Russians would at least be able to equal the Americans, but this was simply real bad. Now tomorrow, I expect you to loosen up and let go; you are preaching the mighty Gospel of Jesus Christ. Show me tomorrow that you can do better than this.* You would never believe the difference that made. They came the next day ready to tear the rafters down; they let go with some of the best preaching I have ever heard from freshmen.

My teaching at Zion lasted from 1954-1958. It stopped only because of some unfortunate circumstances that arose between liberals and conservatives among the staff and faculty. As I remember it, the division was about 50/50. My roots were buried too deeply in conservative Pentecost, so I politely gave my notice that I would not be teaching the following year. Several others did the same. Thank God, Zion survived the conflict and continues today producing godly men and women who circle the globe preaching the Gospel. This experience helped me greatly in this *Drive of Faith;* when it became evident that FST was becoming more liberal than my roots would allow, it became easy to give the reigns to others without causing waves. The college I started goes on under godly leadership and a new and different vision; and that is the way it should be with changes of administration. I support FST with tithes, prayers, and best wishes and have never once made derogatory remarks concerning the college.

Faith Bible College International

Chapter 34

The Revelation and Preparation

In the summer of 1958 a new chapter began in the *Drive of Faith*. In the past twelve years of ministry I had sent at least a dozen young people to Zion for an education. Several of them became pastors, missionaries, and Christian educators during their whole lifetime. Now, because my fellowship with Zion Bible Institute was temporarily severed, I needed somewhere to send students. In June, 1958, I seriously heard from heaven informing me that I was to open a college in Old Orchard Beach where I pastored. I quickly shrugged it off thinking it must be a product of my own mind. For several weeks I kept pushing it away.

Richard and Alice Small were part of my church family at that time. Unbeknown to me, Alice was having devotions by herself one morning in June of 1958, when she felt the Lord speaking to her heart about a Bible college in Old Orchard Beach. She wrote the message on a piece of yellow paper and tucked it away in her dresser drawer. She never told or shared that with anyone until she heard me make an announcement in September, 1958. At the same time, another deacon's wife, Sister Johnson, was resting after her three girls had left for school. Sitting in her easy chair with the Bible open on her lap, a vision of brick buildings passed before her eyes and the thought of a Bible college in Old Orchard Beach came dancing through her mind. Like Alice, she never told anyone until after she heard it publicly.

One morning during the summer of 1958, I received a call from the pastor of the Assembly of God in Haverhill, Massachusetts. He was a graduate of Zion when I was teaching there. His words were something like this; *Brother Pier, I had a dream about you two weeks ago and can't get it out of my mind. I saw you in a Bible school in your town. Is there any possibility of that?* Needless to say, I was flabbergasted and speechless for a moment. I do not remember what I answered, but I know my words kept him guessing. I neither affirmed it nor denied it. This call made me wonder some more if such a far out idea was really coming from heaven.

The following is important and should be inserted here. I hesitate to give any details as this came to me second hand. I do not doubt it as I know the one who told me was a godly saint. Sister Christine Gibson, the president and founder of Zion Bible College, was traveling with Rev. May Miller from Aroostook County, Maine, back to Rhode Island. They stopped overnight at Eden Rest, 74 Washington Ave., Old Orchard Beach. This date was a few months (not more than a year) before Sister Gibson left for heaven in May of 1955. The morning after their stop-over at Eden Rest, Sister Gibson told Sister Miller that an inspiration had come to her about Old Orchard Beach. Her words were something like this; *May, I feel that God is going to have a training place here in this town.* She did not mention it as a school, only the words *training place.* Nothing more was said as far as I know, but four years later Faith School of Theology began *training* young people in a hotel building across the street from where Sister Gibson had the revelation. One could easily stand on Eden's back porch and heave a stone across the street striking the building where we first educated dedicated men and women for ministry – 88 Union Ave.

Doris and I prayed every day concerning such a far out, seemingly extreme idea for two young people (I was only 32 at the time). We had no money or anywhere to turn for funds to begin such a project. I was not fighting God but just doubting if the vision was from Him. It was in the month of September, 1958, that Doris and I knew the idea had come from the heart of God. We knew we were to prepare to open the *Faith School of Theology* in the fall of 1959.

In the month of September, 1958, I had the privilege to announce on 3 different occasions the opening of the college planned for the fall of 1959. The first time was in my church, again at a district youth rally in Southern Maine, and at a fellowship meeting of several different churches in Maine. Immediately, when the name *Faith School of Theology* was mentioned to all three congregations, the Holy Spirit broke forth with a powerful witness. The message always put His approval and encouragement on what we were about to begin. God's endorsement came, as the Scripture says, *in the mouth of two or three witnesses.*

It was clear to see, that from our acquaintance at Eastern Bible Institute, our youthful marriage, the transfer to Zion Bible Institute, our eighteen month stint as a chef in Zion, our pioneer days to establish a church where they said it could not be done, my four years as a professor in Zion, the deep roots in conservative Pentecost that caused me to leave Zion, and a host of other training circumstances along the way that a divine *Drive of Faith* was at work in the hearts and lives of Russell and Doris Pier. Faith School of Theology is a college that God breathed into being. Some preachers predicted it would last for two or three years and go defunct. Those preachers are now in heaven and the college, after sixty years, continues to educate workers for God's Kingdom.

During that winter I worked on putting together a brochure. I wrote for catalogs from various Pentecostal colleges and studied nearly a dozen of those before developing the curriculum I felt would please the Lord. I gave it the name, *Faith School of Theology;* it was to be a school relying on *faith in God;* it was an educational institution so I included the word *school;* and, of all things, it was to be an education in the things of God (theology) with His Word as its main text Book.

Much time was given to creating a logo that would properly describe what the school would stand for. Perhaps it was because I had studied Latin, but at any rate, the words inserted in the round circle on each side of a triangle came out in that language as Fides, Veritus, Spiritus. These were to become the three standard bearers of the school.

Fides is the Latin for *faith;* the Holy Spirit made it plain that I was to train God's servants to trust Him at all times, in all situations. Veritas is the Latin for *truth;* again the Holy Spirit made it extra plain to me that I was to stress the literal interpretation of the Word in our teaching of heart holiness that could be seen in our daily lives. Spiritus is the Latin for *spiritual things;* once more the Holy Spirit made it plain that I was to teach students how to give the Holy Spirit charge of every service, that the Gifts of the Spirit were for every believer and should be manifested often in their lives. As a result, we never had a dead chapel service and the Holy Spirit often interrupted our classes and daily programs along this *Drive of Faith*.

From the beginning of my ministry I was an old-time holiness preacher. As such, in the 50s and 60s I received many calls to preach revivals, camp meetings, and conventions because of my stand for conservative Pentecostal values that are in the Word telling people how they should talk, what kind of appearance a child of God should manifest, where they should be seen and not be seen, etc. Holiness preachers saw these things as a reflection of what was in the heart.

This was the core and main objective for opening this college. The Holy Spirit impressed me that this college was to be different because of its stand against the worldliness that was beginning to permeate the Pentecostal movement. Faith School of Theology was not opened primarily to spread the Gospel; that was one of the side effects. It was easy to see in those days that the world had found a place to bring its fashions, entertainment, etc. into the church; Pentecostals were following their denominational sisters and becoming much like other protestant movements. This college in the *Drive of Faith* was to be purposely different.

After much prayer, I contacted these five individuals asking them to serve as a Board of Directors and trustees with Doris and me for the school: Walter Monroe (school teacher), Richard Small (University graduate and office manager in the Portland Water District), Daniel Johnson (Bible college graduate), Rev. Elva Valerius (University graduate, pastor, school teacher), and Rev. Wentworth Pier (pastor). A town lawyer drew up the papers and incorporated us as the Faith School of Theology in York County and town of Old Orchard Beach, Maine. Every charter member was educated and filled with the Holy Spirit.

This Board met and chose me as its president, Rev. Doris Pier as vice president, and Rev. Elva Valerius as Secretary/treasurer. We met to consider validating applications from those desiring to be students during the spring and summer of 1959. Serious prayers ascended for a place to house these students. We could possibly use the church for a classroom, kitchen, and dining; but there would be no room for residents.

It was at that time I drove by the corner of Washington and Union Avenue in our town and took notice of a three story rooming house for sale. Windows were boarded and a long side porch was rotting and falling apart. A sign gave the name of the owner and his telephone number; Donald Taylor, Limerick, Maine, etc. I called him and arranged a time to see him at his home. There was a real estate dealer who attended our church that offered to go with me. He knew four different ways we could obtain the property without laying out money. We pulled into the drive of Donald Taylor in Limerick mid-morning in the month of June, 1959. As we did, a young man was coming out of the house with a suitcase in his hand. His father was behind him saying his good bye. When his father realized what we were there for, he called to his son who was getting ready to drive to his home in New Jersey. His call said, *Come back here, son. This is something you should hear.* He then explained to us that his son was part owner in the property we were considering.

We sat together in the parlor area as the first floor had no partitions. My friend, the real estate dealer, explained all four suggestions to which Mr. Taylor said, *not interested.* It looked hopeless until we stood up and started across the kitchen floor for the door. Suddenly, the Holy Spirit spoke to me and I turned and said, *Mr. Taylor, would you consider letting me have that property without a dime on the table; I'll pay you six percent interest* (high at that time) *every four months, and in four years I will pay it off?* He quickly turned to his son and said, *that sounds all right to me, yes, we will do that.* I learned on this *Drive of Faith* that God, the Holy Ghost, could do more in seconds than all the efforts man could put forth in hours.

After the deed was in our hands, work began on 88 Union Avenue. My brother, Stewart, spent the summer with me and rented rooms in the building we were working on. Small amounts of money were given towards the new college amounting to about $1,500 including the rent we received. Brother Robert Stevenson, who operated a local plumbing business (a member of our church), offered to install new plumbing in the kitchen, bathrooms, and a new hot water heating system on all three floors. Brother Arnold Day (a licensed electrician and member of our church) helped with the plumbing, and with all the electrical work. Others, both men and women, pitched in for many hours in the evenings to paint, wall-paper, and clean. Everyone discovered in this *Drive of Faith* that there is a lot of work that goes with living by faith.

88 Union Avenue, Old Orchard Beach

Chapter 35

A Faith College Opens Its Doors

The first of October they began to arrive; twenty five students from Maine, New York, Canada, Massachusetts, and other states. Some were parents with children; a single dad with his ten year old daughter, one couple with a son, one couple with three children, and one couple with two children. Several youth out of New York City discovered the coast of Maine in Old Orchard Beach. None of us at the time realized that we were part of a *Drive of Faith.*

Sister Rose Blanchett, a beautician from Saco (member of our church), gave up her business to come and be our matron in charge of keeping the building clean and do our buying. Rev. Elva Valerius gave up pastoring to become a teacher and Dean of Women. A student's wife and mother of three children became our cook. Many others made sacrifices to help us as teachers. Doris and I taught many of the courses.

It was a beautiful sight when we all gathered in the basement church at the corner of Atlantic Ave. and Third St. The Faith Tabernacle rang with shouts and praises in a packed house. Music and testimonies were heard from the new students. God came to visit with us that evening; none of us will ever forget. Gifts of the Spirit were in operation and divine blessing fell on all attendees.

88 Union Avenue in Old Orchard Beach became a busy place in October of 1959. Three meals a day were prepared and served by faith. Students were asked to bring ten dollars each and anything else they could give was appreciated. The money was used for food, heat, electric, and any

other bills involved with the operation of the college. The *Drive of Faith* continued as we all learned each day to pray for God's provision.

In the first week of November that year, Brother Stevenson, our plumber presented me with a bill for the heating and plumbing equipment. The complete wholesale price came to thirty seven hundred dollars. We had fifteen hundred from room rents and gifts that was saved for the project. I assured Brother Stevenson we would have the balance of twenty two hundred shortly. It was a shouting day at the college that same week when Rev. May Miller drove up and parked her cream colored Pontiac across the street. She had just sold the Beth Shan Missionary Home in Lynn, MA, and felt the money was God's money to be distributed for a righteous cause. She had no way of knowing what our need was, but when she handed the check to Rev. Elva Valerius, our treasurer, it was exactly twenty two hundred dollars. What a joy it was to hurry to the phone and tell Brother Stevenson to stop by for his money to pay the wholesale supplier, New England Pipe, in Biddeford. The *Drive of Faith* was shifting gears and moving in the right direction.

There are so many stories of faith answers during that first year, it could fill several pages. One of those came early one morning as I was teaching in the dining room, the only room we had for a class. My desk and chair were within inches of the serving window from the kitchen. The serving windows were closed and I could not hear the cook and Sister Blanchett, our buyer, in the kitchen planning their grocery list for the day. Together they laid their hands on the list and prayed for one hundred dollars to go to the store. It was at that moment that the secretary brought me the mail while I was in class because she thought I might like to see it immediately. Sure enough, there was a letter from my colleague, Pastor Lloyd Sparks in Brooklyn, NY. Inside was a check from his church for one hundred dollars. The two ladies in the kitchen were nearly in tears, rejoicing for God's provision. Every week we watched the *Drive of Faith* as we fed hungry mouths, paid bills, etc. and saw God provide supernaturally.

Faith School of Theology, from its beginning, was not interested in changing Pentecostal convictions to fit the culture of its day. Pentecostals were more interested in living by Bible standards in those days. When I went to Valley Forge University (Eastern Bible Institute – A/G) in 1942, the lifestyle standards were quite simple. Ladies dressed like ladies with skirts and dresses below the knees and jewelry (except for engagement or wedding rings, symbols of commitment) and cosmetics were not allowed; tight pants on men were a no-no and shirts were always part of men's attire. Zion Bible Institute (North Point Bible College) under the leadership of President Christine Gibson, was much the same as Eastern when Doris and I transferred there in 1943. It remained the same until after Sister Gibson's passing. The lifestyle we learned at those colleges had a life-long effect on this *Drive of Faith.*

Both colleges had a uniform dress for classes and services on Sunday. Dress shirts, tie, well pressed pants and suitcoats were part of men's attire on Sunday. Women wore long sleeved navy blue dresses below the knee, starched white collars and cuffs, and a red bow with the collar. Bowling allies, movie houses (theaters), and other such worldly entertainment were out of the question. Strict standards of social rules were observed in both colleges. Both colleges were in the business of training spiritual leaders and they realized how important it was to produce *disciplined* graduates.

With this background and sound teaching from the pages of Holy Writ, you can easily see why similar patterns were introduced at the Faith School of Theology when it opened its doors in 1959 and this *Drive of Faith* continued. Students were looked at as men and women old enough to accept authority and live by rules and regulations, not like little boys and girls who want their own say in how they dress and what they do. We believed Ben Franklin's phrase as we had our lights out at 10 PM and every student was out of bed at 6 AM. In both colleges we had 14 hour a week duty and the more affluent could not get out of duties by paying for it. Again, we all understood that rules and regulations were what we would live by the rest of our lives; the Scriptures are full of such. You don't give little babies rules and regulations; those are for men and women of character.

God helped us to weather the storm of criticism and rejection. During the first year of college I was invited by Pastor Gene Kimball of Charleston Pentecostal Church to minister with a group of singers from FST. That was the beginning of a tremendous relationship and at this writing the pastor of that church (Dr. Matthew Ward, one of my own graduates) is the president of the college. At that first meeting in 1959 the church gave us a beautiful love offering and a man donated a freezer that served the college for many years.

On the flip side of the coin, we ran into difficulty when the pastor of the Assembly of God in Fryeburg, ME, invited our choir to minister in his church. The office of the Northern New England Assemblies of God notified the pastor in Fryeburg that he must cancel with us. Since it was a dependent church, it was important for him to obey. As a result, I was given an invitation to meet with the Directors of the Assemblies. I was interrogated for 2 hours one afternoon. I do not remember the details or even the subjects that came up during our discussion, but one matter has never left me. They wanted to know what our stand was on 1 Cor. 14:27 as they had heard we allowed more than 3 messages in tongues during one service. These were important days and meetings along the highway of the *Drive of Faith*.

Several days after our meeting the Superintendent called me to say that we would not be allowed to minister among the Assembly of God churches. I accepted that without retaliation as the will of God. However a dear friend of mine informed me sometime later that the minutes of that meeting with the Assemblies read somewhat different. The actual wording was somewhat like this; *Because of the uncertainty at this time, we do not feel that we can fellowship with Faith School of Theology at present but we look forward to the time when that will change. Furthermore, Brother Russell Pier will be given respect in any of our services.* It was only a year or two after that when the wall between us crumbled and the college has enjoyed great fellowship with the Assemblies ever since. The Assembly Officials have granted the college special love offerings from their Northern New England office several times.

During the time when the walls were up, I was invited to minister in both the afternoon and evening service in Orange, MA at a Southern New England district fellowship meeting. Students with me sang and testified. However, at their minister's meeting between services someone brought up the problem the Northern New England Assemblies were having recognizing the college. The presbyter informed me before the evening service that the offering would have to go to home missions at which I let him know I was delighted. The Holy Ghost came down in that evening service when I was preaching in such blessing that the presbyter got up himself and took an offering for the college. God has given us great friends among the Assemblies of God nationwide and also with the Church of God everywhere. The fellowship of these and other branches of the Pentecostal movement have been a tremendous blessing to the *Drive of Faith*.

The next summer we knew we needed to expand at 88 Union Avenue. The old porch was torn off and construction began on a two story addition to the east side of the hotel. My figures may be slightly off, but it was about 50 feet long and 12 or 14 feet wide. The first floor was for a chapel/classroom and the second floor was for staff quarters. If my memory serves me correctly, Robert Gogan was the foreman on this job. Bob was the president of the first graduating class of 1962, taught in our college in the 1980s, and always was a great blessing to me personally in this *Drive of Faith*. The next summer (1961) construction began on the old barn connected to the rear of the hotel. We changed it into a classroom and library with dorm rooms on the second floor.

During the third summer we partitioned the long chapel to make two classrooms. We designated the smaller classroom for a ladies prayer room during the evening hours. One night, after lights out, about four or five ladies were in that prayer room praying down the glory. Suddenly they felt the presence of evil and began to rebuke any spirit that might be trying to interfere with their prayers. After praying like that for a few moments, suddenly the lights went out and no one was near the switch. Hysterically the ladies charged out of the room, across the front porch, and up the stairs to their dorm. Needless to say, the dorm was awakened and Dean Valerius came out of her room in her robe to calm them all down.

It was the talk of the school the next day until someone figured it out. There were two switches for the lights, one in the ladies prayer room and one in the other classroom. One of the young men was praying in the larger classroom and left for his dorm, turned the lights off without realizing it cut the lights off in the ladies prayer room at the same time. It was a good time to teach the students on demon power as we needed to do several times along this *Drive of Faith*.

Chapter 36

Our Last Years at Old Orchard Beach

The year 1964 was pivotal. During the first 5 years of the college's history I pastored the Faith Tabernacle (legally incorporated as the First Pentecostal Church of Old Orchard Beach) and carried on my responsibilities as president and professor at Faith School of Theology. In the spring of 1964 I realized it was time to devote my full time to the college. It was growing and getting established as a viable institution of Pentecostal learning throughout the North East. It has been interesting on this *Drive of Faith* to fall in line with changes at the right time.

The choice was given to the church; continue as a part of Faith School of Theology or choose a different pastor and begin independently from the college. An Assembly of God pastor was called to candidate from Schenectady, NY. He was installed late in the month of June, 1964. When the students returned in the fall, I was faced with a problem. We had always insisted that our students attend the local Pentecostal Church where I pastored so they could observe and learn the ways of the Spirit in worship, preaching, and all things needed during a service. To me, hands on experience and observation have always been important on this *Drive of Faith.*

The problem arose, however, when so many of the college juniors and seniors did not care for the new pastor's style. Every pastor has their own style of leadership, and rightfully so, but there was so much difference the students had a difficult time entering into the services. I tried to see both sides of the picture; here was a group of students from the local Pentecostal college sitting there with arms folded and scowls waiting for the last Amen. This created a problem for the new pastor, and I did not want to give him any problem with our unhappy students. So, with unhappy pastor and unhappy students, what shall we do?

The church and new pastor understood that when I got through as the pastor, I divorced myself from the church as I feel all pastors should do. I refused calls and did not attend any services after the installation of the new pastor. When problems came up later between the church and the pastor, I was sure glad I had made a complete separation. Both the church and the pastor felt I should have stood for their side, but I remained completely neutral; an important lesson for all my students on this *Drive of Faith*.

It would not be good for the students to drift around to Non-Pentecostal churches, so I sought the Lord for an answer. It was then that I felt to have a Sunday afternoon service in the school chapel for students and staff only. To sum this whole matter up, the church decided to change pastors in the summer of 1965 and I started looking for a place to move the college to a community where there would not be a college/church conflict.

It was during this time when the pastor and student crisis developed that 3 or 4 of our students were walking in Ocean Park, a suburb of Old Orchard Beach. They were actually off limits when they passed by a Catholic convent where 22 young nuns were studying to be teachers. Amazingly, the nuns asked our students to come in and during their conversation the two groups of college scholars developed a rapport. The mid 60s was the height of ecumenicity when Catholics and Protestants were trying to find common ground.

The results of this happenstance meeting was an official invitation from the convent to send a committee of 4 or 5 students to meet with a committee of nuns and plan a service together in their chapel. I handpicked students for the consultation which resulted in our student body traveling to the convent one evening to worship with the Catholics. The committee planned the service with a song from a Catholic hymnal and a song from ours. Their choir sang and our choir sang. The nuns on the committee asked our students what we did in our services and they told them that we had testimonies of the goodness of God from different worshippers. The nuns were not used to that but wanted our students to plan for 3 or 4 testimonies.

When the songs were chosen the nuns insisted on everyone singing our song; *I'll Fly Away, Oh, Glory; I'll Fly Away.*

It was a blessed night as we gathered, sang, prayed, testified, listened to choirs, and worshipped. I do not remember that they did any preaching. I will share an interesting side episode that took place. One of our lady students (whom I will fictiously refer to as *Wanita)* did not want to go, but I insisted she come with the whole body. While walking from the Catholic chapel to their dining hall where we had refreshments, one of the nuns walking with Wanita, grabbed her arm and pulled her into one of the classrooms and shut the door. She quickly asked Wanita about this speaking in tongues. She insisted she tell her as she was very interested. Needless to say, as quickly as possible, Wanita shared her own experience of being filled with the Holy Spirit. This is something that so often happens on this *Drive of Faith;* Christians sometimes balk at something that God has planned, and those in leadership have to use their authority to lovingly insist.

While mentioning Wanita, another little incident comes to mind. This is the same girl who conned me into going home for a weekend; she did not actually lie to me but made the situation sound like it was necessary. I did not want to, but I gave in and let her go. She told me years later that after the Sunday night service at her church, she and another girl were sitting in front of the Dairy Queen licking their cones. They had the radio tuned to a station where a preacher often gave prophecies, and suddenly this is what came over the air waves; *This is Pastor Al in Hayward, California.* (suddenly during his message, he stopped and said) *You young lady, home from Bible college on pretense,* and then proceeded to scold her for such action. She was sitting at a Dairy Queen at 10 or 11 o'clock on Sunday evening in the State of Maine, and someone in California told her off. This *Drive of Faith* has had several comparable incidents.

There was excitement in the air the next Sunday afternoon after our service at the convent. The local Catholic Convent came to worship with us at the Faith School of Theology, 88 Union Ave. All 22 nuns were there with Mother Superior and her aide. They walked into our humble abode, down the entrance hall, and into our dining room where we held service. Chairs were all set up and our students were present to give them a loving welcome. We had an ordinary service with songs, choruses, testimonies, etc. There was Pentecostal worship as we raised our hands, praised the Lord, and messages in tongues, interpretations, and a prophecy came forth.

When it was time to preach, I read the text and delivered a message about the Cross of Christ. I concentrated on truth I knew they would be familiar with. They were very attentive and seemed to enjoy each part of the service.

We had a lovely chicken dinner ready after the service. Mother Superior sat at my table with her aide. We discussed some of the service when suddenly she asked a question I had never been asked; *That young man that spoke in other tongues – speaking in tongues is in the Scriptures, so I don't doubt it, but he seemed like he was in pain or suffering while he gave that message?* I smiled to myself as I have seen some giving messages that wrinkled up their face and it might appear that it was a bit painful to be giving a message in other tongues.

I assured her that there was no pain or suffering, but that when one senses the power of another world, this physical might react in that fashion. I have used this story many times since when teaching about the Gift of Divers Kinds of Tongues on this *Drive of Faith*. In fact, I have taught a number of times that believers when they use their gifts should relax. The shaking, screwed up facial expressions, and other physical reactions are not the Holy Spirit; these take place simply because those believers are not completely yielded. I remember when I was a student in Bible college that I would grab on to the sides of my seat in church when I started giving messages in tongues. I would nearly shake the chair to pieces, and I thought, *My, the power of God is so strong I can hardly stand it.* Lessons like this come everywhere along this *Drive of Faith*. Believer with your gift, learn to yield completely to the Holy Ghost and you will be surprised at how wonderful is the flow of the Spirit.

Our time together with the Catholics ended and we never saw or heard from them again. I found out sometime later that one of our young male students said something to one or more of the nuns just as they were leaving, something that wasn't called for. I still remember that young man's name, but I never found out what he said. I blamed myself (remember, the buck stops here) for not having educated the students sufficiently before the nuns came. Those young ladies were wholly committed to their cause; they had taken pledges never to marry and to devote their entire lives to the work of their church. That takes dedication few of us possess. It may be for a cause we do not agree with, but it is dedication just the same. May those of us who walk this *Drive of Faith* take notice and learn.

Two things were challenging me; some people were visiting our Sunday afternoon service and I did not want to start another church. The other reason was enough in itself to search for a new location for the college; we were at capacity for room; 53 students filled every nook and corner at 88 Union Avenue. Several began to pray with me. Some, however, felt there was something sacred about the college beginning in Old Orchard Beach and to move we could be out of God's will.

And so the search began; New England, New Jersey, Pennsylvania, New York? I made a trip to Chambersburg, Pennsylvania to tour through a large set of vacant buildings previously used by the city for public schools. Another trip took us to New Hampshire to consider a summer camp with several buildings. These searches, along with other offers, were prayed over.

One of these quests seemed very promising. Someone told me of a State owned TB sanatorium in Hebron, Maine, that closed in 1959 (the very year that FST was founded). There was an apple orchard of several acres, a large dairy barn, a large brick administration building, a Cape Cod style home for the administrator, and several wooden buildings for patients. I went there with some on my team and it appeared to have potential for our needs. We could actually make enough from the apples each year to partially operate the college.

Since it was owned by the State of Maine, it would need an act of the legislature to dispose of it. I made several trips personally to Augusta; sat and talked with the legislators of that district and convinced them to send a bill to the floor of the house for a transfer of the property to Faith School of

Theology. It got an affirmative vote and was sent to Governor Reid for his signature.

A basket of apples was brought to the campus in Old Orchard Beach and passed out to students and staff as *fruit like the grapes of Eschol in the Promised Land.* Many hours of prayer went up as we stretched forth our faith; this could be such a blessing to our young fledging college. On this *Drive of Faith* there have been several times when challenges rose and blessings appeared that would meet the need only to discover God had bigger and better plans.

The Governor and his council vetoed the bill; in other words they turned it down. No reason was given and I never did try to find out what became of that property. However, when I announced the Governor's decision in one of the classes, the Holy Spirit immediately responded with a message in tongues and interpretation. I do not remember the exact wording, but the impression it left with me was that *God had something better in mind.* The Spirit of God immediately gave me the Scripture from 1 Thess. 2:18; *We would have come unto you, even I Paul, once and again; but Satan hindered us.* I figured if Satan could hinder a giant of the faith like the Apostle Paul, it should be no wonder that he could do the same to little ole me.

Chapter 37

The Move to the Brooklin Campus

And so the search continued with a trip to Cape Cod. It was the summer of '66 when Pastor Marion Kendricks invited me to speak on a holiday weekend at the Dennisport Pentecostal Church. God arranged it for me to lodge with the Pastor and her husband. We talked extensively about relocating the college and he asked me to stay on Monday morning before leaving for Maine. He took me to a real estate dealer where the dealer gave me a real estate magazine entitled *Century* with hundreds of properties all over the North East. I perused the publication with a prayer for God's guidance which was usual while on this *Drive of Faith*.

That was the magazine in which I discovered a piece of property located in Brooklin, Maine, that had possibilities. It was listed for sale at $155,000. Within the next few days, Doris and I made a trip to Brooklin. We discovered 35 acres of land, of which about 6-8 were lawns. With 126 feet of ocean front, it had been used as summer vacation property. An outdoor saltwater swimming pool, the largest in the State, was on the back lawn. There were 10 two-story buildings scattered about the lawns, including a large administration building bordering the street. It housed a kitchen, dining hall, lounge, staff quarters, etc. The guest buildings would help us double our present enrollment.

The property was under foreclosure with the Gardiner Savings Institution. The real estate man the bank had hired to sell it was in Florida on a 2 week vacation. We were not supposed to find that out, but God had another idea. I made a telephone call after we spent some time praying about the situation and met with the treasurer of the Bank. I asked for the lowest price he would take for the property. He asked several questions about the college and made a final offer. With his hands stretched out on his desk, he said, *Well, I'll tell you Reverend, we have $100,000 in that property.* At that I got up and started for the door stating that there was no use me talking as we had nothing like that to offer. He quickly called me back and asked, *What can you do?* I told him that I did not know, but would talk with my board and make him an offer.

We fasted and prayed and in a few days wrote this offer: *We will give you $15,000 down and sign a mortgage of $35,000 to be paid on monthly.* The next weekend I was a guest speaker in the East Millinocket Assembly of God. The treasure of the bank called the school, found out where I was, and called me in East Millinocket asking me to stop at the bank in Gardner on my way home Monday morning. I remember so well the interesting look on the man's face when I walked in and took a seat across from his desk. Twiddling with his pen up near his face, he looked at me and said, *Reverend, we checked you out, and I want you to know we would not do this for anyone else in the world, but we are going to do it for you.* He then stated that the papers would be ready to pass in 2 weeks. I simply said, *"I'll be here in 2 weeks with the $15,000",* and left for home.

Our directors and student body went to prayer; we did not have $1,500 let alone $15,000. Twelve days passed and no money. It was a Wednesday; I am to meet the bank on Friday. Just before noon on that day, I opened the mailbox in the little Post Office in Old Orchard Beach and lo, and behold, there was an envelope from a Mr. Leighton in Massachusetts. His daughter was a student in our college and evidently she had told him about the need. It was shouting time at the noon dinner table when I relayed the news of a $5,000 dollar check from Bro. Leighton. There have been scores of shouting times along this *Drive of Faith* over the years, for which we thank God and our many friends.

While we were rejoicing, I reminded the Lord (as if He needed someone to remind Him – lol) that $5,000 was not $15,000, and we would need the rest of the money in 2 days. It was Thursday evening while I was sitting in my office when the telephone rang. It was a person-to-person call. The operator said, *Rev. Russell Pier, please.* I assured her she was talking to the right person, at which she said, *Go ahead, mam.* I will never forget the words that came from the other end of that line; *"This is Sister Mildred Wallace in Roseville, Michigan. I understand you need $10,000 to help purchase a new campus for the college"* (her son was a student at our college). I responded with the words, *"Yes, Sister, we do"*. Her next words went like this; *"Well, I want to tell you what happened to us. My husband passed away 2 years ago. We owned some large wheat fields in North Dakota and have been waiting for the estate to be settled. It was settled 2 days ago and I am going to put the $10,000 in the mail tomorrow."*

Some of you may remember that it was a Pastor Robert Wallace that told me I would never have a Pentecostal church in Old Orchard Beach because there was a curse on the chapel property. It is interesting to note that a person by the same last name (Wallace - though no family relation) gave money for me to move the college to another town after the church had been firmly established. The church is still in Old Orchard Beach after 70 years. And the *Drive of Faith* goes on.

True to her word, Monday morning the check arrived. Since the bank in Gardner had not called me the past Friday, I called them on Monday and said, *when you are ready, we are.* The bank gave me the date to come and when I had signed all the papers, I turned to the treasurer and told him the story of Bro. Leighton and Sis. Wallace. He stared at me, bewildered, and said, *"Well, you can certainly call that an answer to prayer".* In all the ten years we had a mortgage with that bank, we were never late one day with the payment. The *Drive of Faith* has helped us over the years to maintain our integrity with the public.

It was an exciting day when the college made the trip in separate cars from Old Orchard Beach to Brooklin in the spring of 1967. The details of that day are rather hazy in my mind, but we spent the day with a picnic lunch as we toured the grounds and buildings of the new campus.

During the winter of 66-67 the campus in Brooklin lay dormant waiting for our moving day. In the month of May, 1967, we received a bill from the town of Brooklin for several hundred dollars; it was a property tax. When I contacted the town office they told me that since we were not using the campus for a school on April 1 (1967) we could be taxed. I doubted their findings, contacted a good lawyer, Mr. Silsby, in Ellsworth, and let him handle it. It took several months to go through the courts but when it was finished the lawyer never charged us a penny. We had won a *land mark case* in the Maine Supreme Court. Blessings like this have always come dancing by our way on this *Drive of Faith.*

Back to Old Orchard Beach it was time for our last graduation, May of 1967. We had been given permission to use the Campground Tabernacle during the past few years for our graduation services. The property had changed hands that year and ownership had passed to the New England Salvation Army. I was instructed that we would not be able to use it anymore for our graduation services. I made a trip to the New England office of the Salvation Army in Boston and talked with the Colonel. He explained to me that the Army had to assure the trustees of the Camp Grounds that they would not let Pentecostal groups use it. He added, *I think that is because they talk in tongues; you do talk in tongues, don't you?* I was quick to answer, *Yes, we do.* I wanted to say, *You bet we do,* but I felt the shorter answer was more appropriate given the setting at the time. With that we wished each other well and I left for Maine. This *Drive of Faith* has always been a strong supporter of worshipping in tongues daily for every Pentecostal believer.

After graduation we rented a semi 18 wheeler with a 40 foot trailer and filled it full for 3 trips to Brooklin. Since I had never driven a semi before, I took Warren Morgan with me to get the truck. Brother Warren was one of our converts and had gone to school for driving semis. He drove it out of the truck yard in Portland, instructing me on the way, and parked it in front of 88 Union Avenue, Old Orchard Beach. Several students worked that summer helping us move and prepare the new campus.

We began loading the trailer at 4 PM and at 4 AM it was completely stuffed. We needed 3 men to help us unload in Brooklin and there was only room in the cab for 2 next to me. Gary Malloy was the student who volunteered to ride in the recliner, sitting by the door in the rear of the trailer. I was not sure how legal it was but that is the way we made the first trip up Route 1 to Bucksport and down the secondary roads to Brooklin. We stopped periodically to check, making sure Gary was safe in the box. He texted me the other day; that trip was over 50 years ago and he is still alive, so I reckon the experience didn't hurt him any. Thank you, Gary, for being that brave volunteer in June, 1967. I have been blessed to have many brave and hardworking students help me along this *Drive of Faith*.

An eventful summer started at the new campus when I backed that 40' trailer up to the main building and the men began unloading at 8 AM. I had overseen all the loading and had not slept all night. Driving a semi for the first time was rather exciting. Brother Warren had explained the 10 gears to me and told me I probably would not drive above 6th gear for a beginner. Truthfully, I was hardly out of Old Orchard Beach on Route 1 before I was in 10th gear having the time of my life. While the men unloaded, I got some shut-eye so I could return the truck later that day and save money.

We had a small utility trailer that I pulled behind my Pontiac that we used to bring incidentals that had not gone on the truck. The little trailer was packed full for our last trip one late afternoon, making it dark before we got to the new campus. It was 167 miles from Old Orchard Beach to Brooklin. Brother Fran Cormier and his family were traveling with us in his vehicle. I had no lights on that utility trailer so when it got dark, Bro. Fran taped a flashlight on the rear of the trailer so the men with blue lights wouldn't stop me.

We had calculated that we needed to build five cellars under existing buildings, purchase and install 13 hot air furnaces, four hot water heaters, and a new submersible pump in the existing well that summer. Frances Cormier was the man who made a great difference for us, and has blessed this preacher many times on this *Drive of Faith*. He was a married man with one or two children when Faith School of Theology opened its doors to educate and prepare him for ministry. When we moved to Brooklin, he was young, about 25, with a brilliant mind of an engineer. There wasn't anything that Fran Cormier could not do. He oversaw the installation of all those furnaces, water heaters, and the new pump in the 195 foot well. He certainly was God's man in God's time on this *Drive of Faith,* and I will be forever grateful for his efforts and friendship.

It was at a breakfast table on a Thursday morning that first summer at our new campus that I asked my team of nearly a dozen men to join me in prayer. We needed $10,000 pronto as I was planning to hire another semi out of Bangor on the next Monday. I had called and made arrangements to pick up all those furnaces, heaters, and supplies at the plumbing company in Portland. We prayed together at the table and left it in God's hands. Two young male students were working with me under the main building erecting cement blocks. I was teaching them how to mix mortar and apply it before lifting each block and putting it in place.

Suddenly the lady student working in the office on first floor came running out on the porch above us and told me I had a long distance call. It was about 10:30 that morning; 3 hours after we had prayed. Dropping the trowel, I rushed upstairs. On the other end of the line was a brother in Massachusetts. He told me that he woke that morning with a message from the Lord to call me; the message was to send me $10,000. True to his word, he sent $11,000 which arrived on Monday; Tuesday morning I was on my way to Bangor and Portland for the equipment we had ordered. Needless to say, there was a shout around the campus that day like so many others along this *Drive of Faith.*

The first winter on the new campus was brutal. The buildings were not insulated and finished off for winter weather. When the students returned from Christmas vacation the first of January, 1968, it was plain to be seen that I needed to make decisions; the college classes and school activity would be practically impossible. Within less than 10 days I sent the students back home for about 6 weeks and moved staff and others who had to stay into one or two buildings. It was within a few days of the first of March when classes began; freezing cold winds, etc. were still present with us. The students tell of taking their mattresses across the dorm hall to the lee side of the building when the wind blew from the opposite direction and switching back to the other side when the wind changed in the next night or two. Hardships such as this have often increased our faith on this pleasant *Drive of Faith.* This extended the spring semester into June when we had our first graduation in Brooklin on the lawn.

While writing this, I was reminded of the high level of graduates that came from that experience. At least two or more of the men and their wives have pastored the churches where they are at present for over 30 years; one man and wife pastored churches, made several trips into Cuba and Mexico, became leaders of a Teen Challenge in a large city; another man is presently working with the Assembly of God National Headquarters while traveling as a musician; Rev. Pearl Wells and Faith Bell still work on our college campus since becoming students 1967. Only eternity will disclose what kind of Christian Marines came out of those classes in 1968-1970. We have some terrific graduates on the fields around the world, but I don't think any of them supersede the graduates of that era.

We were concerned about the windows and began to pray for some storm windows to seal out the cold and the wind. That year, while we were having the difficulty with the cold, a widow lady in the Boston area passed away. Bertha Andrews was a personal friend of Doris and me; she had stayed in our home in Old Orchard Beach on two different occasions. Before passing from this life, another personal friend of mine, Pastor John Fitzgerald of Roxbury (suburb of Boston) went to the hospital to see Sister Andrews. She had several thousand dollars that the State would have received if she did not have a proper will; she did not have one single living relative. Rev. Fitzgerald arranged for Sister Andrew's lawyer to meet them at the hospital and she dictated a will and signed it within hours of passing. She divided the money between my Alma Mater, Zion Bible Institute, and Faith School of Theology. Several months later our college received a check for about $23,000 which helped us purchase storm windows. Once more, on this *Drive of Faith,* God came through with provisions just in time.

Brooklin campus - 1967

Chapter 38

Eight Years of Life At The Brooklin Campus

W e held our next closing convention and graduation in the local Baptist Church. We were able to negotiate its use through Rev. Sidebottom, the local Baptist pastor. However, Pastor Sidebottom visited part of our service when God was moving in a supernatural way. Rev. Bill Wilson from Mars Hill, Maine, was the preacher and as usual, Bill prayed the glory down. The blessing fell that night so students were dancing up and down the aisles and God's presence was so strong. The Pastor was concerned about the floor giving way and told me this kind of service was unacceptable. This *Drive of Faith* has seen hundreds of meetings that would never be understood by the natural mind.

As a result, the whole campus gathered the next morning in the empty swimming pool that had a floor with a perfect pitch for a church floor. The pool measured 110'X45'. We walked around praising God and claiming a tabernacle building. Rev. Bill Wilson was one of my best friends; he preached the baccalaureate when I graduated from Zion (1945), ministered several times in our Old Orchard Beach church, and served on the Board of Directors of Faith School of Theology. That morning in the empty swimming pool he made a statement I have never forgotten; *I am sure God showed Brother Pier where this Brooklin property was, as He was the only One who knew.* Bro. Wilson prayed a prayer that morning that was full of faith and sure enough, God began to move.

That summer God touched the heart of Tony, an Italian builder in Long Island, NY. He came to our campus and built both the temple over that swimming pool and my home on the campus. He discovered a wife among our students and I married them; the first and only marriage in the church he built. Some of us will never forget Tony and his bus that he used to pass out tracts and be a witness. It was the night before everyone was leaving for Christmas vacation. Tony was going to drive his bus home, but he had to get it out of the snowbank and ice. The student men were helping him by pushing. It appeared that his tires were frozen in the ice, so they took pails of hot water and tried to thaw out the tires. They must have worked more than an hour, pushing and heaving, but it wouldn't move an inch. Finally they gave up for the night.

In the morning they were all flabbergasted and a bit upset, even though they were laughing a long time when they found out the answer. The bus was not stuck; Tony had forgotten to release the emergency brake. Tony was such a likeable fella and he will never be forgotten in our story of this *Drive of Faith.*

Our staff changed during the first few months on the new campus. Sister Rose Blanchett, who had been with us most of the years we were in Old Orchard Beach, did not feel to leave her home in Saco and relocate with us in Brooklin. Some of the local teachers and helpers were the same. My sister, Ruth Jones, moved from Western New York State with her three children and became our cook for the next 20 years. Her motherly ways got her to be known as *Ma Jones.* Her daughter, Kathy, came at the same time as a college student.

Excellent teachers commuted from New Hampshire, Southern Maine, and churches in Central Maine. Pastors George Hendrickson and James Peters carpooled to drive nearly 200 miles each week as professors. Other pastors became our convention and daily chapel services.

One of my closest brothers, Milton Lloyd, came as a gardener and handy man, eventually becoming the teacher of sign language in the college. His boys, Kenneth, Thomas, and Kelvin, came with him. We did not know about Christian schools or home schooling at the time, so my daughter and her cousins from both of these families became students in the public school at Brooklin; the high school young people traveled to Blue Hill Academy, about 12 miles north. Both Milton and Ruth had unfortunate marriage situations, so they were working with me at the college without their partners.

I have been blessed on this *Drive of Faith* to have every one of my siblings working with me at one time or another. Wentworth was a charter member of the Board of Directors; Ruth was the longest tenure; Milton was second only to Ruth; Bill was with me for many years, not only in Brooklin and Charleston, but in Nigeria, Kenya, and Florida; Mary's husband graduated from our college and they both worked on the Charleston campus; Pam served as a teacher on the Florida campus; and my youngest brother taught in Charleston and Baltimore. I am forever indebted to wonderful siblings who devoted their time and efforts without thinking of money.

We used every idea that we could think of to provide food. We developed a garden spot that the neighbor made available across the Naskeag Point Road from the campus. We made a potato cellar under part of the dining room in the main building where we stored tons of potatoes shipped from Aroostook County farmers. It was some sight to see the long semi back up to the outside hatch cellar door. The student men made a basket brigade and passed them to each other, filling the cellar with some of the best potatoes in the world. We were blessed many years on this *Drive of Faith* with potatoes and vegetables from farmers in Washburn, Presque Isle, Mars Hill, Caribou and other Northern Maine communities.

Four men and one lady car-pooled and drove the 50 miles from Bangor every day for classes; at least 3 of them graduated and spent their entire lives in ministry. At lunch hour, they were often seen at the horse shoe pits challenging students and staff.

Visitors came from near and far to attend our Sunday afternoon meetings and conventions. Who can forget Bro. Dotson, Bro. and Sis. Nevels, and several others who joined us for the blessings of a Pentecostal service on the Lord's Day? Before we built the swimming pool chapel, we had services at the Naskeag Point chapel about a mile from our campus. We had at least one water baptismal service in the ocean at the end of Naskeag Point Road.

It was in the middle of February during a blizzard that I had the honor of tying the wedding knot for the renowned Bill and Joyce Parks; two graduates I am fondly proud of. They chose the Rock Bound Chapel about 3 or 4 miles from the Brooklin campus. Their families came from Pennsylvania and Maryland; needless to say, they had a brutal, cold Maine weather welcome. When I performed weddings, I like to make their day special with something they would never forget (for instance, I tied my brother, Bill, to a tree out in the woods during his wedding reception and took Bro. Elliston Smith for ice cream right after his wedding ceremony). You see, I liked to make sure each couple had something memorable that would be hard to forget. Because of that, I made this story about Bill and Joyce part of this *Drive of Faith* book.

Bill Parks knew about my shenanigans so he hid his car 12 miles away in Blue Hill before the wedding. However, when his best man delivered him to his vehicle, he found he had left the keys to his car back on campus in his dresser drawer. The blizzard was so bad that no one wanted to take him the 12 miles back to the campus for his keys. He was left with an alternative he never expected; he called me to bring him the keys. He knew snow storms did not bother me, so he made the call.

I will never forget the first words that came from my mouth; "Bill, you are not going to give me the blessing of waiting a couple of hours, or perhaps dangling the keys inside my locked Pontiac while you stand there in a blinding blizzard of snow and ice, are you?" I prayed earnestly and felt compassion for a couple that was to become so special among my graduates – spending their lives pastoring and building a great church, plus making several trips into Mexico and Cuba. Eventually Bill became the Director of Teen Challenge in Baltimore, MD, the city where he grew up fighting on the streets.

On the Brooklin campus our students lived in several different buildings on the second floor with staff members on the first floor. Male scholars had their habitat over our family living space. It was my blessing to spend a few moments with the men upstairs on several occasions; I had a great desire to make well-disciplined spiritual Marines out of them. For that reason, I insisted on the kind of daily regimen I received in college that instilled in me the kind of character that has followed my life on this *Drive of Faith*. Rules and regulations do not bother mature Christians; they submit with loyalty to their superiors.

All of our students knew that 10 PM was a long enough day; all lights were to be out and the bed was their resting place for the night. One evening I felt to check on my Marines after 10, so I tiptoed upstairs and listened at each doorway for any that were misbehaving. Two or three bunks occupied some rooms; lights were all out and everything seemed quiet. Just as I left and started for the stairway, I heard something strange. I listened more intently and heard the perk of a coffee maker. I spoke to the faking sleepers and discovered there was a coffee maker they had shoved under the bed when they heard me coming. I do not remember how it ended but I am sure those men will never forget. One thing for sure; they knew I loved them and whatever happened was for their good. Discipline with love was always important on this *Drive of Faith*.

On another occasion, Jose Valcarcel, an anointed singer and student in one of those rooms upstairs, returned late from traveling with me on ministry. One of his dorm mates was adept with electric and sound equipment. He rigged up a tape recorder on the floor under Jose's bunk with a connection to a lamp in the corner of the room. It had a switch under Jose's pillow. All was quiet as Jose got into is PJ's in the dark and crawled into bed. When he laid his head on the pillow, the lamp went on and the recorder started playing. Jose jumped up and when his head left the pillow, the lamp went out and recorder stopped. He got back in bed and again the light went on and recorder began to blast. Jose came to as to what was happening as pandemonium broke out in the dorm with laughter coming from every bunk. Need I say anymore? Again, there was always some kind of excitement as we trained these young lives along this *Drive of Faith*.

Jesse and Shirley Jones drove their company bus with several friends all the way from Washington, NC, to at least one of the graduations. The Joneses, Tates, and Gurganuses made the 971 mile trip to be present at our graduation ceremonies in our partly completed swimming pool chapel. Here is the story told by Jim, son of Brother and Sister Gurganus, This kind of tale has often been repeated along the *Drive of Faith*.

> *My dad was less than enthusiastic about me going to a nondescript school in a nondescript town in Maine after graduating from NC State Univ. The physical condition of the campus gave dad no reason to change his mind. On graduation day, you asked dad to get some men together and become an Usher group to escort all parents/guests to their seats. This is something dad, a natural leader, did in short order.*
>
> *A few minutes after the service began dad was getting concerned. Hundreds and hundreds had shown up and been seated, including all the ushers, and now there were only 3 chairs left in the pool/tabernacle; one next to mom for himself and 2 others. A couple walked up, dad seated them and then sat down concerned what he was going to do when others, he knew had to be coming, showed up.*
>
> *After a while dad slowly began to realize....no one else was coming. Dad wept that day, not because of what the speaker said, but because of what God did that day, He filled EVERY seat with none left over! Concerning all things Church, dad felt all things should be done decently, in order and in an excellent manner. God reached him where it counted. From that day forward dad became one of you and the School's most ardent advocates, and remained so until he passed.*

The following happened in the spring of 1975 when our dorms were filled to capacity with 115 students. We had 90 students that would be arriving as freshmen in the fall. We had to have more dormitory space to continue our *Drive of Faith*. Here is another story Jim reminded me about, told again in his own words.

We were maxed out at the Brooklin Campus and you asked me to get a set of dormitory building blueprints from NC State. I contacted my advisor and he sent basic blueprints of the Bragaw Hall Dormitory Bldg. that I had stayed in. It was a 4 story brick building laid out in the shape of an 'X'.

Sometime later we were having a service in the pool/tabernacle and you asked for testimonies. Sue Landerville stood up and spoke of a dream she believed was from God concerning the Faith School Campus. In it she saw a large multi-storied brick building. You shared that the process had already begun to look into the erection of a new multi-story brick dormitory....God Willing! It eventually became apparent that Sue was not seeing the Brooklin Campus (all wooden bldgs.), but rather the Charleston Campus.

Chapter 39

The Charleston Miracle

S omeone had given us a large bull dozer and I had fired it up, prepared to dig a hole for the foundation of a new dormitory on our Brooklin campus in the spring of 1975. Our largest enrollment was about to descend upon us that fall; where would we put over 90 freshmen? We had reached capacity – 113 students in the spring of that year. The blueprints lay before me and as soon as the frost was out of the ground, I was ready to place that bulldozer blade in the sod.

In the month of March, I received a red light stop sign from heaven. I did not argue with God; that is one of the most stupid things a man can do, but I did let Him know I was bewildered. What kind of a miracle would He be thinking of for the enlargement of our dorm space? God kept me waiting (I was trying to be patient with Him) until the last of April when my good friend, Glendon Faloon, called with a suggestion; *Did you know that the Higgins Classical Institute in Charleston was closing?* Brother Faloon suggested I contact the Directors of that property and negotiate a purchase.

Higgins Classical Institute was an academy founded by Rev. John Higgins in 1891 as a college for the training of ministers. It had some connection in its early years with Colby College in Waterville. The vision to train ministers only lasted a few years at which time the campus became the home of an academy for high school students. I cite all of this to say how elated we felt to be continuing the vision of Rev. Higgins nearly 85 years after the school's founding. We have oft been made to wonder how many prayers in past generations this *Drive of Faith* may have answered.

Had I lost all my marbles to listen to this suggestion from Brother Faloon? Higgins Classical Institute was a 35 acre campus with a full sized football field, gymnasium, administration building with offices, chapel, and several classrooms, 2 dormitory buildings, staff duplex home, modern ranch style principal's house, large coal fired boiler room with an 80 foot smoke stack, etc. It was valued by an insurance company at 1.5 million dollars and I understand the trustees turned down an offer of over $600,000.

Faith rose in my heart and I made an appointment to look over the property. They allowed me to come and tour with a promise in my pocket no one knew about from the Book of Joshua; *Every place that the sole of your foot shall tread upon, that have I given unto you.* I realized the promise was to Joshua but God clipped it out of chapter one and gave it to me.

In the evening of the day I toured the campus, the trustees of Higgins Classical Institute asked to meet with me. They had several questions about the college and I told them exactly how it was. They asked about a budget; I replied, *how can we have a budget when we do not know how much money we will have? Today we have $5,000 in the bank, tomorrow it has been reduced to $50. When a need arises, we take it to God in prayer and He has never failed to provide for the past 16 years; every bill has been paid.*

Pastor Ronald Libby was a member of their trustees and I am sure his word went a long way to convince them it would be good for the town to have our college on the property. Pastor Libby had known us since the beginning of the college in 1959 and became one of my best friends for life. He served many years as a director on the board of Faith School of Theology and was a great friend of the college and my wife and me on this *Drive of Faith.*

Higgins trustees asked me to wait in the hall while they deliberated and voted. I doubt if it was more than five or ten minutes before they called me back in. I do not remember any of the exact words they used, but in essence the chairman of their trustees said they wanted us to have the property with a couple of stipulations. The property had a mortgage of $45,000 which we were to assume and they would like it understood that any high school graduate living in Charleston could attend Faith School of

Theology free of any tuition charge. I was sure our directors would have no problem with that, and so the date was set for a turnover of the property.

It was the last week of June, 1975, when the trustees of Higgins Classical Institute met with our directors in the Institute Building on their campus. It was a beautiful and awesome sight to see these men and women ready to end one phase of the Institute's work and begin another. Chairman Leon Williams called the meeting to order. One of Higgin's trustees moved that all of Faith School of Theology's directors be accepted as trustees of Higgins Classical Institute. The move was seconded and the affirmative vote was unanimously cast at which time each Higgin's trustee signed their resignation. Within a moment of time the directors of Faith School of Theology had become the owners of the campus of Higgins Classical Institute. One more giant step on this *Drive of Faith.*

A scary moment at the close of the meeting took place when the former principal suggested, *"Don't you think that Rev. Pier ought to give some money to the Higgins scholarship fund in lieu of this transaction?"* Judge Silsby, a member of Higgins Trustees, spoke up immediately, *"Oh, no, there must not be a dime on the table or the IRS will be in here and we will have all kinds of problems".* That settled it all for those present. And what a relief it was for me to hear those words; one more blessing along this journey on the *Drive of Faith.*

God blessed us with a great crew that summer of 1975. Every one of them was a real worker and ready to help in any area needed. I am reluctant to name any for fear of leaving someone out. Car loads and truck loads of staff's personal belongings, plus office and college supplies were moved week after week. Facilities on the new campus had to be arranged for each staff member and work had to be done to change rooms into small (some just 2 rooms) apartments for new staff.

At the same time, renovations such as painting inside and out were orchestrated at Higgins Classical Institute. One of our students offered to come and engineer the removal of the huge coal fire boiler in the furnace building next to the tall brick smoke stack. I am not sure of which summers some of the work was done, but during the first couple of years wooden buildings were painted, a freezer room was built, oil fired boilers were installed for some buildings, roofs were patched, and a host of other things costing tens of thousands of dollars.

The move from Brooklin to Charleston was a giant step of faith. Where the money came from, I do not remember, but we made history on this journey; the *Drive of Faith* had found its final resting place. It still continues under great new leadership to touch the world for Christ. One of the greatest blessings was the mortgage money of $75,000 loaned us by Christian Mutual Insurance Company. This was presented to CMI by my special friend, Glendon K. Faloon, a graduate of FST and one of their insurance salesmen. That loan helped us pay off the $45,000 mortgage we assumed with the transfer of the property to our name and install a new efficient boiler in place of the antiquated ark we inherited.

The first five years in Charleston were the busiest of any time in the history of the school. Purchase and renovations of a large home with several acres of land on the northwest corner of the Main and School Road intersection, and the Post Office building on the southeast corner of the same crossroads was involved. This was to house the increased enrollment at that time; between 150-200 students. It was interesting to see some at meetings where I told about feeding well over 200 three times a day and not know where the next meal would come from. I remember a lady rubbing her hands together and exclaiming, *I wouldn't know what to do for such a crowd without knowing what to cook for them.* And so it was for decades on this *Drive of Faith;* beloved, I can assure you we never went hungry. The God who gave manna in the wilderness is still alive and ready to feed those who trust Him; have you watched a sparrow lately?

There were some great moments to see God work miraculously during those first years in Charleston. We developed a great relationship with Pastor Ronnie Libby and the Charleston Pentecostal Church from the start go. Sometime during our first year Pastor Libby asked me to preach each Wednesday evening at their midweek service. I have always felt that was a special honor to work with that great man of God.

The oil and electric bills were huge. A telephone system needed installation to connect those whose positions made it necessary to often contact each other. We built a root cellar to keep our truck load of potatoes from Aroostook and other vegetables from freezing. Two or three acres were plowed up and planted with vegetables. A garden tractor, lawnmower, snow plow, etc. were needed; all costing plenty of money. More dorm cots were purchased and many repairs to the property caused our faith to be stretched. But, after all, that is what this *Drive of Faith* is all about.

The driveways needed patching and flowers had to be planted. It was beautiful to see everyone work together, planting, picking, freezing, hammering nails, roofing, etc. In the meantime, we were all concerned with the sale of the Brooklin property. Some Brooklin business men got together and offered us $50,000 which we quickly rejected. They upped their offer considerably when they realized we could sell it to someone who could develop it into low-cost apartments and they would have (what they would call *undesirables*) as neighbors. I do not remember the exact price for which we sold it. The sale helped make us debt free and to travel on with this *Drive of Faith*.

Peter Chase, the former principal of Higgins Classical Institute, came to see me the first or second week the college opened in Charleston. I was involved with something in the office, so he waited in the hall. This was just at the time when the bell rang for chapel to begin. Students were coming down the stairs from classes and entering the chapel next to where he was standing. He observed their behavior and happy faces. Chapel began with beautiful singing just as he was called into my office.

Peter Chase was a self-proclaimed agnostic. His first words to me were, *My, there is a different spirit in this place.* After leaving my office, he went to Mrs. Tracey's home next door. She was the wife of the principal before Mr. Chase, the man for which the brick dormitory was named, *Tracey Hall.* She had been one of the directors who voted for us to have the property. She told me personally, *Rev. Pier, Peter came in all excited. He told me I must go visit your chapel service, there is something electrifying going on.* He recognized the whole atmosphere was charged with the presence of the Mighty God of Heaven.

I arranged for teams to walk with their Bibles through every dorm and building, cleansing them with pleading the Blood of Christ. So, of course the atmosphere had changed from a drug infected culture to a holiness campus that did not even have a television.

Mr. Lester Francoeur, the owner of the only store in town told someone that it was so different when our students visited his business. *I don't have to watch and make sure they are not stealing like I used to do. They are polite and such a different group than the young people of last year,* he said. Some of the locals did not like it because I wouldn't allow them to have their ball games on our ball field on Sunday, but all in all, the community accepted us with gladness and love. We did make arrangements with a Mr. Fitzgerald in Atkinson, a town just north of Charleston. He owned a field large enough for playing ball next to the local grade school in our town. We traded woodland Higgins Institute owned for that field and had him deed it to the town of Charleston. This gave the locals a chance to develop a beautiful ball field and have their games on Sunday.

It is difficult to know where to begin writing about the great days on the Higgin's property, but perhaps I should start with the chapel. It was easy to see from the start that the chapel in the institute building was too small for Pentecostal worship. In prayer, I was led to consider a new chapel that would blend in with the other buildings on campus. We contacted the new owners of the Brooklin property where we had built a chapel over the swimming pool. We discovered they had no use for the chapel (110x45) and would happy to have us remove it. We sent a team with our college truck and piece by piece it was taken apart and reconstructed at our campus in Charleston.

It was a summer project. Several of our students stayed and gave their time and effort to this endeavor in exchange for their utility fee the following school year. I would include their names as they were some of the best, but I'm not sure I remember every one and I would not want to miss some and cause any offense. If my memory serves me correctly, I believe the entire project from beginning to end was carried out by our own men. In other words, we took that temple apart, loaded it on a truck, transported it the 75 miles to Charleston and rebuilt it by the same dimensions.

On this *Drive of Faith,* we have seldom hired outside help. God granted us helpers that knew what they were doing and developed in us talents we did not know we had. When you trust God, it is amazing what he can teach you. I cite this, not to boast, but to encourage younger faith loving pioneers on a similar *Drive of Faith*; I had never worked with a carpenter or builder and knew only what I had observed and read in books I purchased or inquired of those older than I who had done the work.

It has been a blessing during my young ministry to install electric wiring single handed in an old church that had none; lay out foundations with a line level, Plumb Bob, and something I sighted through over distance (I do not remember the name of it); lay hundreds of cement blocks; mix the cement with a small electric operated 10 shovel mixer and pour concrete footers; do I need to go on with hanging 12 foot pieces of sheet rock single handed with a "dead man," lay floor tile, roof a building with shingles, etc.? Young people, you can do almost anything when you are building for God's kingdom and have faith to believe Him.

The new chapel was erected in front of the gymnasium between Tracey Hall and the Institute building. The reason I put it there was to construct hall ways around the outside wall of the Chapel, connecting all three existing buildings. This made it unnecessary for anyone to walk outside during the cold winter to get to classrooms, gymnasium, or dining hall when traveling from building to building. Construction was still going on when classes began; rafters and side walls were up but the roof had not been installed yet.

Chapter 40

The Elva Valerius Chapel And Its Miracles

It was in the winter, I'm guessing, some weekend in January that I traveled to Danbury, CT for a weekend of services. Pastor Manzer Wright of the Assembly of God in Danbury had called me to minister in the church he pastored. Pastor Wright was a long-time friend of mine and it was in answer to his prayers that our college landed in Charleston on the Higgin's property. He was at one time the pastor of the Assembly of God in Dover Foxcroft about 12 miles north of Charleston. One morning, not too long before we knew about Higgins, Pastor Wright pulled his car over to the side of the road in front of the school buildings and prayed. He was passing through Charleston when he felt led of the Spirit to pray for that property. He had some strong feelings that God had a plan for Higgins.

After the service in Danbury Sunday evening, I drove back to the college in Maine. The sun was just coming around when I drove up in front of the property. During the night, Charleston had a heavy snow storm. Wet snow had piled up on the slate roof of the Institute building. Before I arrived the snow piles had let go and slid down the slate striking the first rafter on the new chapel we were reconstructing. Like dominos, one rafter leaned into the next and so forth until ever rafter let go taking the side walls with them and the building lay practically flat on the cement foundation.

As I turned the corner to enter the college drive, I began to shout, literally shout, Hallelujah! Praise God! I knew that was abnormal; I should have been crying, but the Scripture I have lived by on this *Drive of Faith* suddenly became alive, *I will bless the Lord at all times, His praise shall forever be in my mouth.* I did not understand that any more than you do, but I knew it was the thing to do.

How we approached this in chapel and to the directors, I do not remember. It was nearly two weeks after the event when my friend and faithful staff member, Rev. Frank Godley, checked with our insurance company and discovered we had construction insurance on that new building. The end of the story is that we received over $25,000 for the damage done by the storm. We had no money to finish the building and prayers had been sent up to help us complete the construction. The money from the insurance was enough for us to complete the entire building. To God be the glory; His ways are not our ways. The Elva Valerius Chapel stands on the property today as one of our monuments on this *Drive of Faith.*

Something should be said here about the name I placed on this new chapel. When I first heard of Rev. Elva Valerius, she was the pastor at Dennisport Pentecostal Church on Cape Cod. After a few years in Dennisport, she went to Newburyport, Massachusetts, where she pioneered and built a new church now known as Assembly of God. She was a great woman of faith and those are the kind of people you need with you on a *Drive of Faith.*

Sister Valerius was chosen by yours truly to serve as a charter member on the Board of Directors of our college in 1959. She was approaching 60 years of age at that time. She was a graduate of a college in Massachusetts and had taught school. I am not sure of the year, but when she surrendered her heart to the Lord Jesus, her husband walked away. I may not have the details correct so I won't write much, but she was somewhere in her mid or late 30s when this happened and she pledged herself to a life of celibacy. She believed like I that remarriage under any condition was sinful. In spite of her young age at the time of divorce, her entire life was impeccable.

She was appointed by the college president to serve as the Dean of Women until her passing in 1981. The Directors voted her to serve as the college treasurer and she did a superb job as such for many years. I gave her a large front room on the second floor (ladies dorm) to live in when we began the college in Old Orchard Beach.

When we enlarged the building our second year, we built three rooms as an extension of the second floor; one I gave to Sis. Valerius, another to

Sis. Blanchett, and the room in between they used as a kitchen-sitting area. Both of those ladies were from the elite side of life, and yet were humble enough to accept meager living quarters. I have had many, many such ladies and men who served at our college under similar conditions; such partners were so important on this *Drive of Faith*. Believe me, our present students as well as those over the last 60 years, have little knowledge of the great sacrifices my staff made to make their education possible. The thousands of personal accolades I have received belong to some of the greatest people I have known; those who worked tirelessly by my side on this *Drive of Faith*.

We used the smaller chapel in the Institute building until the large chapel was built and ready for occupancy. Things happened in that little chapel that will never be forgotten. Many times the glory of God would fill that room when students and staff alike were overcome in Pentecostal fashion; chairs were pushed to the sides and as many as 50 at one time could be seen dancing in praises to God; some were prostrate on the floor receiving visions or otherwise inundated with the Holy Ghost; Gifts of the Spirit and ministries galore were demonstrated for hours at a time. Our children in the day school downstairs came up and were praising God, dancing right along with the rest; it was a beautiful sight to behold.

It was shouting time one worship session in September of 1977 when Bro. Ed Asante stood to testify. One of our English students had just given a message in tongues and another had given the interpretation. Bro. Asante's words were something like this; *Bro. Pier, may I testify? My wife and family are home in Ghana being cared for by her parents while I came to get my education. I have not seen them for two years and was hoping I could return for a little while this past summer, but that did not happen. I came into this service sad, missing my family so much. I was in real need for something from God to encourage me. The sister who gave that message in tongues was speaking in the pure dialect of my mother tongue* (there are several dialects in Ghana) *and the interpretation was perfect. This was a great encouragement to me.*

We had some fantastic answers to prayer for food in those days. Prayer was made when I told the 7 AM prayer service that we had no meat for meals that day. Students were faithful to pray earnestly and just as I got to the office about 8:30 the secretary informed me there was a call to answer. I greeted the party with the words, *Good morning.* On the other end of the line, a farmer in Washburn, ME, asked if someone from the school could meet him in Bangor later that morning as he had a side of beef he had butchered and wanted to donate it for our tables. Many an Aroostook farmer came to our rescue in those days and the college will be forever grateful for their needed help.

We had a similar need in the early 1980s when we received a call from a fisherman on Swans Island, ME. He said that he had 500 extra pounds of frozen lobster meat he would like to donate. What a blessing; in weeks that followed and there was little to eat, we would say, *Lets have lobster from the freezer!* While there were a few who did not have a taste for lobster, there were many of us that felt blessed to be eating with the upper echelon.

In the spring of 1975, while we were contemplating enlarging the campus, we discovered the Accelerated Christian Education vision that Dr. Donald and Esther Howard were developing in Texas. It appeared to be an opportunity to start a Christian school with Christian curriculum in our own church; in our case, in our college program. An application was sent to the ACE office in Texas. Arrangements were made for Brother James Ansara and me to fly to Texas and spend 5 days to be trained in the ACE program. This was required before we could use their curriculum and start our day school.

The bottom line is that Higgins Classical Institute became an educational institution for grades K-12. The carpenters on my staff and summer students went to work building corrals for each Higgin's student that would be applying. Basement rooms were painted and decorated, teacher's desks and equipment were moved in place, and in the fall of 1975 we had about 25 students. HCI became useful in the training of our Bible college students who were majoring in Christian Education. They received hands on training in the classrooms.

It was a beautiful sight to see the students in red, white, and blue uniforms day after day being trained in a Christian education. There were times when they joined us in the college chapel service where they saw firsthand the moving of God's Holy Spirit in Pentecostal fashion. When special times of God's blessing fell, one could see children dancing in the Spirit with college students; some of those precious youngsters received the Baptism of the Holy Spirit. It was a sad day for me when Higgins Classical Institute could not continue, but I thank God for the trophies among our HCI graduates that are still in active ministry as of this date. This was not the only bitter/sweet incident along this *Drive of Faith*.

In retrospect, I can see that the personal training and infusing of my vision into the leaders that would follow me was more important than I realized. If my life lasts long enough, I would like to write a program for others to use so that it could help future leaders; perhaps they would have less bitter/sweets than those that came to me. Higgins Classical Institute and at least 6 Bible colleges that I helped start are defunct. That does not make me happy, but when the training and infusing of vision was lacking, one has to accept the consequences. If you are a leader on your own *Faith Drive*, pay attention to this paragraph. I have asked God to anoint this section for some reader that seriously needs it.

It was somewhere near the first of August our first years in Charleston that our summer workers had been living on rice and pasta with their vegetables, fruits, and meat. We were taking prayer requests as usual directly after supper. One of the students said, *Brother Pier, can't we ask God for some potatoes instead of the rice and pasta?* My answer was in the affirmative and we talked to God immediately.

We had no sooner got off our knees when the telephone on the first floor just above us was ringing. One of the ladies ran to answer. She came back and told me the person calling desired to speak with Brother Pier. I walked up stairs and found a man named Malcolm Dunfee on the other end of the line. His message was something like this; *Brother Pier, Could the school use some potatoes? I have just purchased a lot here on the Beans Mill Road in Corinth. They are coming in next week to bulldoze a hole where my house will sit and it is right in the middle of a potato patch. I hate to see all those good potatoes plowed under. If some of the students want to dig them out, you are welcome to them.*

What a lesson for anyone on a *Drive of Faith*. God has different ways of supplying our needs but he does not always serve them on a platter. There have been a number of times like this when God has implied, *Come and get it if you want it!* Our students and staff took their shoes and socks off, and worked hard in the mud and dirt to dig out several bushel of potatoes that lasted us until the annual truck arrived from farmers in Aroostook.

Chapter 41

Colleges Open In Other Locations

It was in the early years of the 1980s that Rev. Ed Shobanke of Abeokuta, Nigeria, got in touch with me. He came and spent some time at the Charleston campus and requested that we start a Faith School of Theology in Nigeria. My missionary brother, William (Bill) Pier, Sr., agreed to go with his wife and start the college. Bill was able to raise his support and spent the beginning years until he was replaced by John and Naomi Patton. Other graduates were sent to help these leaders and several preachers and teachers were produced in Abeokuta. I made the trip and preached the first graduation.

Beloved, there was a deep cry in the hearts of many Pentecostal millions during the 1980s. A new and different Pentecost was taking over in America and being exported to other countries. I am writing from a broken heart when I tell you that we lost the battle. Pentecostal preachers came to me from several countries begging for a Pentecostal college in their country that would hold the line against the worldly changes of this generation. Bro. Shobanke (Nigeria), Bro. Douglas (Jamaica), Sister Betty (Panama), Bro. Molefe (South Africa), and pastors in Russia, Kenya, Alberta and New Brunswick Canada, and Mexico are some of the places efforts were made or at least a visit to determine possibilities. Some of the leaders told me of American supported Pentecostal colleges in their country where they sent their youth for training. These same young people returned to their churches and tore down the holiness teaching with American worldly ideas taught in college.

It was my privilege to minister in 4 different Russian speaking churches in Utica, NY one weekend. Thirteen Russian pastors and leaders met with me that Sunday afternoon. They were given copies of the Faith School Theology catalogue and my Russian interpreter explained each section in their language. I saw them turn toward each other with grins, shaking their heads. My interpreter explained to me that they found it hard to believe that there was a college in America that taught a life of heart holiness that is seen in the lifestyle like Pentecostal believers in Russia. It was after that meeting that Professor Frank Shaw and I made a trip to Russia and taught some 30 students for 2 weeks in one of their churches.

It was in the early 1980s that it seemed right, after serious prayer, to search for a location in Canada to open a Faith School of Theology. We had trained many Canadians at our Charleston campus and had a good relationship with a multitude of Canadian churches. I accepted an invitation to go with Brother Mark Blakney and look at an empty school building in the Province of New Brunswick.

The property was not suitable for a resident college campus so we returned to Mill Cove where I was staying overnight with Pastor and Sister Luther Blakney. During our conversation that evening, Pastor Blakney suggested that I consider the church property where he was the pastor for a Canadian Faith School of Theology. He explained in detail the property complex; the church owned two parsonages and the sanctuary on a few acres of land bordering Route 105 just off the Trans Canada Highway. Pastor Blakney wanted life right to the parsonage he lived in but was willing for us to use the bedrooms upstairs. There was room in the sanctuary basement for dining and classrooms. Some student rooms could be arranged in the basement of the recently built parsonage up the hill in back of the sanctuary. I did not waste any time to proceed with the offer and in February of 1984 a meeting of trustees was arranged.

Rev. Frank Godley, Rev. James Shuelke, Secretary Pearl Wells, and my wife made the trip to Chipman, NB, to meet with the said trustees. There was less than 6 or 7 people considered trustees, but many others were present (about 21) as there was great interest in our vision. Rev. Luther Blakney called the meeting to order. When brief preliminaries were over, the chair entertained a motion to accept Dr. Russell Pier as a trustee of the corporation.

Motion was seconded and carried with unanimous vote. At that point, all the other trustees submitted their resignations with a signed statement. This was all done on purpose so that I could choose my own board of trustees and use the property according to the vision I had previously described. I chose 4 Canadians and 4 Americans to serve with me as the chairman.

The 5 of us left Chipman in a snowstorm late that night. We had no problems until we crossed Route 16 on the road leading into Bradford about 10 miles from home. That road had not been plowed and we were pushing snow up over the car's hood. There was no alternative except to install the new set of wheel chains I had purchased a few days before. I was the only one who had boots so out I went. It had been several years since I had worked with a set of chains but I did remember some important things. Needless to say, there I was, nearly 60 years old, on my knees and eventually on my back in the middle of the unplowed road after 2 o'clock in the morning. In due time the chains were snuggly fastened and we were praising the Lord on our way home.

The summer of 1984 was a busy one in Canada. Rev. Jeffrey Bell and his wife, Faith, were installed as pastors in the church at Mill cove. Carpenters in the church went to work on the church basement and the parsonage to make room for students to live. Advertisements went out for students and staff needed. Reconstruction was finished, staff was obtained, and students were on their way. These new recruits graced the class room in the fall of 1984 and Faith School of Theology of Canada was founded.

Great stories of faith can be told about the FST of Canada under the ministry of one of the finest men I know, Dr. Jeffrey A. Bell. His wife, Faith Di Bonaventura Bell, stood ably by his side and worked like a Trojan throughout the many years they pioneered the Canadian college. At the same time, during the 1980s, it was my pleasure to link up with Pastor Gary Heffler in Baltimore, MD. Both Dr. Juanita (Kehl) Golding and Dr. Stewart V. Pier helped me pioneer an FST of Maryland where several students were educated during its brief existence. A college was pioneered in Kingston, Jamaica, with Pastor Douglas and the help of Wally Farmer and his wife,

Brother Green, David Brittenricker and his wife, and Christopher Hutchinson. Some graduates of that college are in the ministry at this writing.

In 1988 it became possible to pioneer a college on Bible Camp Road in Groveland, FL. This part of the story is told with a great deal of emotion surging within my breast. Doris had just had lumpectomy and received a good prognosis. Boxes were packed and truck was hired. During the Christmas break tires rolled and we were on our way to the sunny south. If you are curious about my emotions, let me just say that this part of the *Drive of Faith* would be much different if I had been free to fulfill the vision God gave me for a Faith School of Theology in Florida.

In the spring of 1988, my brother Bill and I made a trip to Florida. I was convinced in my heart that the Holy Spirit would lead us to the right property for a Faith School of Theology in that State. The pastor and people of the North Side Assembly of God in Tampa had welcomed me with open arms. Their church building was available for classes, meals, chapel, etc. We investigated property next door for a possible dormitory, but we could see this was not to be. The pastor introduced us to Brother and Sister Munson on Tampa's outskirts. They lived in a beautiful ranch style home surrounded by 12 rented house trailers. After long discussions, we discovered this was not the property God had in mind. Bill and I were leaving for the airport when I received a message from one of our graduates who begged us to look at property in Groveland before we made a decision. I assured him I would keep it in mind and proceeded on the trip for a flight to Pensacola, FL, where a school building was for sale. But Bill and I could tell that was not God's plan.

Back to Tampa and over to Groveland sometime in mid-afternoon was our last hope before returning to Maine. We drove to the property at 5800 Bible Camp Road owned by John Jennings. My graduate had given us the address and here we stood on pine needles under huge trees and looked with God's eyes on 13 acres of land with several buildings. Nothing we had seen compared with the potential we envisioned at this site. While we were standing there news came that John Jennings was on a train ride across Canada. Senior citizens could purchase a ticket at half price and ride from

Nova Scotia to British Colombia, a beautiful scenic tour. He would not be returning for several days and we could not remain in Florida more than another day.

Bill and I knelt in the pine needles and looked up toward heaven as I prayed something like these simple words: Father, this property appears to be your plan for a Faith School of Theology. Would you please confirm it by sending John Jennings back tomorrow? In Jesus name, Amen.

The next day, the very next day, Bill and I drove on the property, got out of the car, and walked on the same pine needles where I had prayed the day before. We noticed an Airstream Travel Trailer that was not there before. Just then a man appeared alone coming from the trailer and walking toward us. When he was within hearing distance, I called out, *Mr. Jennings.* He answered, *Yes.* I said, *John Jennings?* And he answered again, *That's me.*

"I thought you were in Canada", came from my lips, to which he answered, "I was until last night when my wife called me and told me there was a problem in the business I run and I needed to get back as soon as possible". At that point he told us how he had arrived in Toronto and asked for a train through NYC to Florida. Train connections were impossible without him staying over a day in NYC and he needed to get back as soon as possible. He called the airlines and booked a flight to Florida, took care of his business problem, and came out to see his property in Groveland.

I pointed at the pine needles beneath his feet and told him about my prayer yesterday afternoon. He said facetiously, *So you are the one who disrupted my trip.* After we exchanged words about ourselves, we got down to business.

In the next few weeks a deed, mortgage, and an agreement was drawn up and signed by both parties. John Jennings and his wife made a special trip to Charleston, Maine and met with our directors who would be involved in this transaction. The directors of Faith School of Theology voted and gave me the authority to proceed with establishing a campus for the Faith School of Theology of Florida.

Rev. Bill Pier, Sr.

Chapter 42

Florida College Begins and Ends

My brother, Bill, and others worked together preparing the property for the first classes in January of 1989. Ten junior students at the Charleston campus volunteered to help us pioneer the new college in Groveland, Florida. They left Charleston when the school closed for Christmas vacation in 1988 and started classes in Florida when we opened the first part of January, 1989.

We accepted about 10 or 12 new students as freshmen. My faculty consisted of Rev. Doris Pier, Rev. Marcy Pier, Rev. Pearl Wells, Sister Pamela Ringer, and Rev. Joseph Landerville. The next fall when we had all three years to teach, we added Dr. Bruce Clark and Rev. Michael and Joanne Richard. One more campus on this *Drive of Faith* was in the making. Canada, Jamaica, Nigeria, and Baltimore had been started and now Groveland, Florida. South Africa, Kenya, and Russia were soon to knock on our doors.

In the meantime, I appointed Rev. Timothy Shaw to take my place as leader in Charleston. Brother Shaw moved into the ranch home I lived in and took over my office in the Institute building. He arranged the faculty and staff and did a fantastic job for three years. We kept in constant contact with each other.

During the 7 semesters the Florida college was open we established a church with weekly services where several were saved, a Christian Academy where children were trained, a fourth year college program, and graduated several preachers and teachers that are still in ministry. Church contacts were made and fellowship established in the area. While in Tampa I was able to develop a friendship with Brother and Sister Munson in North Tampa that resulted in several thousand dollars willed to the Charleston campus at their passing. While it was one of the saddest days of my life when we turned the Florida campus back to Bro. Jennings, all was not lost and the blessing continues today as the *Drive of Faith* moves on.

We had an interesting experience on super-bowl Sunday in 1989. We had only been in Groveland for a few weeks and were looking for a Pentecostal church that was open on Sunday night. My station wagon was full of staff and students and we had driven to several towns without success. We were on our way home as it was after 7 when we came upon a church of our faith in Zephyrhills. The parking lot was full of cars and the church was well lit. I stopped and everyone got out with me. I was the first in the door but was surprised to find this beautiful sanctuary empty except for two elderly ladies sitting half way down the aisle. I asked them where everyone was and they quietly told me that the congregation was downstairs watching the super bowl game. I do not remember my exact words, but they probably were, *"You gotta be kidding"*.

All of us quickly left the building, amazed that our Pentecostal churches had fallen so low. Our forefathers in the 1940s would turn over in their graves had they known the future generation would desecrate the Lord's Day in a Pentecostal church building in such a manner. We soon found out that it was customary in Pentecostal churches throughout the State; many of them felt it was proper to use a church building for this purpose even though it had been dedicated to God. Our churches in Maine were still holding Sunday night services. We were aware that some had backslidden so far as to stay home from church on the Sunday night of super bowl, but I am quite sure none had ever attended a nationally televised ball game in the church. Such an experience helped us all to know how important it was for the *Drive of Faith* to establish a holiness Bible college in Florida.

It was not long after that when we started having Sunday services on our campus. It was beautiful to watch our students and those who worshipped with us being moved by the Holy Spirit as God visited each service with His unique divine presence. Do I need to remind you that there is a heavenly connection between the lifestyle church people live and the old fashioned Gospel meetings where the Holy Ghost showed up in gifts of the Spirit and demonstrations of His power? Scores of times during the latter years of this *Drive of Faith* I have been blessed by those who constantly remind me of the Holy Ghost services we used to have. My answer to them is a reminder of the Biblical lifestyle Pentecostals respected and enjoyed in those days.

During the 4½ years the Florida college was open, there were countless times when supernatural provision came from the hand of God. One of the most dramatic happened one morning about 10:30 as I was walking from my dwelling up to the classroom. Sister Patty Jollotta was the cook and she met me there on the lawn with a question; *Brother Pier, what are we going to have for lunch today?* I asked her what she had and her answer was, *some potatoes, onions, and milk.* The two of us bowed our heads and openly asked God for His provision after which each of us went our way. We had just done what we always did at such times on this *Drive of Faith.*

Within a few moments, everyone on campus heard Aubrey Jollotta, the cook's son, hollering at the top of his lungs, *I got it, I got it, I got it.* Brother Ringer was the first to reach Aubrey who was standing on the wooden dock at the edge of the lake. 10 year old Aubrey had cast his fishing line into the lake and had a fish he was having a hard time to bring in. Brother Ringer grabbed the line and ran up the lawn dragging a 7 pound bass on Aubrey's fish hook. Brother Ringer unhooked the fish, carried it out on the dock, took out his pen knife and was cleaning the fish. Just then he looked down in the water by the dock and saw another bass. He quickly took a piece of the insides of the fish he was cutting, put it on the fishhook nearby and dropped it down in front of the fish in the water.

The rest of the story is a part of history on this *Drive of Faith.* That was a 5 pound mate he pulled from the water and both fish ended up on our dinner table with some milk, potatoes, and onions to make some of the most delicious fish chowder you could ask for. We were feeding about 20-30 people and had plenty to go around. The sequel to this makes it more of a miracle when you consider several of the males on campus could not catch a fish of any size in Lake Catherine for at least 2 weeks after that fish chowder incident.

There were many more faith testing times during those years at the Florida campus. We dare not mention names as I am sure we would miss some, but every single person who helped us during those years is sincerely appreciated. Several graduates of the previous years or their parents came to our doors with provisions or sent them via USP. The *Drive of Faith* had established the beginnings of another college campus that was destined to be short lived because of difficulties beyond my control. In retrospect I should never have left Groveland but circumstances seemed to make it impossible for me to remain in the place of my calling. Writing this story has made me search the Scripture for one of God's servants who passed through a similar struggle.

In the spring of 1991 Brother Timothy Shaw felt his time had come to move on to another ministry. The *Drive of Faith* was about to face a challenging crisis. For the first time in its 30 year history the Faith School of Theology had to search for a new leader. It was difficult enough to find someone who could manage a college, but when you add the fact that it was a *faith* college it multiplied the problem.

I called the directors to meet in Pastor Stearn's office in Nashua, NH. We were at least 2 hours earnestly considering a new supervisor who would be willing to fill Bro. Shaw's shoes. No one on the board of directors felt the call of God in that direction. The meeting ended in a stalemate with a decision for me to spend two weeks in Florida and two weeks in Charleston each month, maintaining both campuses. I enjoy traveling, flying, etc., so I reluctantly agreed. I knew I was not to leave Florida campus as it was too young in existence to expect someone else to take over.

Sometime during the summer of 1991, Bro. Jeffery Bell, the headmaster of our Canadian Faith School of Theology, came to me with an offer. I wanted him to consider leading the Charleston campus since Bro. Shaw had left, but he did not feel he was ready for that position. He felt, however, that it was too much for me to travel and carry the load of both colleges. His offer was to leave Canada in the hands of Rev. Randy Crozier

240

and move to Florida to lead the college in Groveland. I thanked him for the offer; he has been more than a son to me since his graduation from FST in 1978. I hesitated before accepting his proposal; *would this be the right direction to take the Drive of Faith?*

There are details too many to print about the transition in 1991. I will give you two or three of the critical ones that laid heavy on my heart.

1. Dr. and Sis. Bell had done a colossal job at pioneering the Canadian college; I was not at ease about them moving.
2. The Florida college was less than 3 years old and had heavy financial responsibilities.
3. The most difficult of all was leaving what I felt was God's plan. I knew my future was at the Florida campus and I had absolutely no desire to return to Maine. My whole life on this *Drive of Faith* had been in the pioneering field. That was and still is my forte. Pioneering started a month after my graduation from Zion when I opened a mission in the city of Pawtucket, RI, and has involved nearly 50 projects during the many years of my ministry.

To return to Charleston was not easy. What does a man do when he knows what God called him to do but things do not fall in place to accomplish it? It is a mean position to be in. My wife was tickled pink to return to Maine, the directors could not find another competent leader for Charleston, and everywhere my head turned there were questions. You can believe it when I tell you it was the most difficult struggle I ever had on this *Drive of Faith.*

Chapter 43

The Season Ends for the Drive of Faith

T he decade of the nineties was destined to become the time for change and an end to this great journey. *To everything there is a season, and a time to every purpose under the heaven;* that was the declaration by a wise man in ancient times. The *Drive of Faith* began with a person, found its fruition in 1959 when Faith School of Theology was breathed into being, and ended its season in the nineties.

Change was not optional; it was required if the college was to be a viable institution in the new church style of the coming generation. This change must have new leadership that could blend the old with the new and not cause more turbulence than necessary in the Pentecostal seas. I was aware that hundreds who had been influenced by my deep-seated conservative views would not understand. My prayer is that the section I am writing now will aid those who need it and give them a loving heartfelt peace.

It was necessary for me to make changes in the staff upon my return to Charleston. I immediately started to prayerfully search for a leader to take oversight of the college. I knew my season was ending and the leader to follow the founder of any institution should have special qualifications. I was well aware of the turbulence that came when Sis. Gibson passed away at the end of my first year of teaching at Zion Bible Institute. The struggle we had at Faith School of Theology was not much different. When the dust settled at the end of the decade, my choice to fill the position of leadership was in place. Dr. Jeffrey A. Bell had worked side by side with me from the day he graduated from Faith in 1978. Like Daniel of old, Dr. Bell had an *excellent spirit* that qualified him for leadership.

There was no question in my mind that many things had to change and I was not the one to do it. I fully supported Dr. Bell as he gently one by one allowed those changes to become part of F.S.T. It was during this decade of the nineties that I begged the Directors to change the name of the college. The leadership had changed, the location had changed, changes were slowly coming to life at the college, and most of all the purpose had changed.

In 1958 I wrote the original purpose stating clearly that the Faith School of Theology was for training Christian leaders to *maintain the conservative holiness lifestyle* of our Pentecostal movement as we spread the Gospel of Jesus Christ. I started preaching in 1943 and had watched the conservative teaching that had been in place for over 30 years in our Pentecostal churches slowly dissipate. I was so thankful when the Directors finally changed the name; I support the new school with all of my heart. My personal convictions have not changed and I still believe and live as I did decades ago, but I accept the fact that everyone does not see it as I do. I understand that the Bible teaches each believer must live by the rules they believe are right; *Happy is he that condemneth not himself in that thing which he alloweth.* The difference is in the way each interprets what God wrote in the Bible.

During the 1990s, after I returned to Charleston, pastors in South Africa, Kenya, Russia, Panama, Mexico, and Saskatchewan (Canada) invited me to explore the possibility of starting a *holiness* Bible college in their country. These pastors did not like what they saw in many of the other Pentecostal Bible colleges in America. When I started Faith School of Theology we lived by the same godly standard set by Eastern Bible Institute when I attended as a freshman in 1942. In those days the Pentecostal churches, as a whole, supported such a lifestyle and expected their future ministers to be educated likewise.

All of this changed over the second half of the last century. In the 1990s there was only a small minority among churches that lived the lifestyle I was taught at Eastern and Zion. That lifestyle is a *conviction* in my spirit, not a *preference*. A conviction is something you will die for; a preference is a "take it or leave it" issue. When I tell people that I have never been in a movie house since I was saved 83 years ago, it is hard for them to believe. Belief is even more difficult when I tell them that I do not watch movies on television. This, and dozens of other issues, separates the modern Pentecostals from the patriarchs of our Pentecostal heritage.

Beloved, this is the reason I felt a God-given desire to step aside and let Faith School of Theology continue under another name with a new vision. I was in my upper 70s and had a wife near 80 who was struggling with health issues. It was time for me to step aside and continue the *Drive of Faith* in a different vehicle. I had seen too many older preachers stay at their posts longer than they should. The Pentecostal church world in general would not support a Bible college that followed the lifestyle of our patriarchs. Again, I emphasize, it was time for change. I insisted on a change without contention. I believe God gave me Dr. Jeffrey Bell to bring about changes gently and lovingly and I am pleased with the success of his efforts. The present president, Dr. Matthew Ward is a star in my crown, one of the many great preachers God helped me train. Together they make a great team. I love them both and pray for them daily.

This is supposed to be the last chapter, but really the closing chapter of this *Drive of Faith* has never been written. It will continue with our graduates until Jesus returns for the *ready ones*. According to Moses, King David, Daniel, Malachi, and the Apostles Paul and John, eternity is full of memories. I believe we will share testimonies and have glad reunions for hundreds, perhaps thousands of years. It was Malachi that wrote, *a book of remembrance was written before him for them that feared the LORD, and that thought upon his name,* 3:16. King David wrote, *Thou tellest my wanderings: put thou my tears into thy bottle: are they not in thy book?* Many other references could be given, but beloved, be assured that our history is recorded in heaven and the only thing blotted out are sins confessed and forgiven; *Repent ye therefore, and be converted, that your sins may be blotted out,* Acts 3:19. Our graduates now have a chance to write their part of the story in this *Drive of Faith* and it will continue on in heavenly chariots throughout eternity.

Until then, as the song writer put it, *I will go on singing*. The music was still playing as the 21st century began and I started winding down my activities at the Faith School of Theology. It was a fateful day in 2001 when my sweetheart fell and broke her foot on our cellar stairs while I was teaching in the Institute Building. Her physical situation deteriorated from that moment on.

I had the honor to care for her at home for 16 months 24/7. It was then for the first time in our married lives I purchased and placed in our home a television monitor. It was not connected to the outside world; it was used only to play DVDs for my wife's enjoyment while I was in class or out of the house. If I had to be gone for an extended period of several hours, I got someone to sit with her.

It was a learning experience to dress her each morning, and prepare her for bed in the evening. I placed her on the potty-chair 2 or 3 times during the night. It became more difficult when I had to obtain a side rail for the bed because she would try to get out of bed by herself when I wasn't near. If she succeeded, she could easily have fallen and broke a hip.

On November 10, 2002, she took wings with the angels and landed on heaven's shore among relatives and friends who had been notified she was coming. The song writer expressed my feelings when these words were written, *I can only imagine.* My granddaughter sang that at Doris' funeral. Thousands had been touched by her life and ministry; she had faithfully served the Lord without ever having a thought of backsliding for 64 years. Over 50 ladies stood at the altar and in the aisles at Glad Tidings in Bangor, Maine, when I challenged them to pick up the prophetic mantle Doris left behind and commit themselves to follow in the wake of the waves her ship had made. My confrere, my co-driver, my teammate, my life-long partner was gone; but the *Drive of Faith* must continue.

2003 began my first year as a single since 1943; what should I do with the remaining years of my life to continue this *Drive of Faith*? I had been teaching in Faith Bible colleges since my first year as professor in Zion, 1954. What could I do with the knowledge I had accumulated during those many years? I felt a burden to continue letting those in this generation know that there was a better way to live the Christian life, a life free from the bondage of worldliness, a life where you did what you wanted to because the heart had been sanctified (separated). My burden also concerned the poor; those like myself that did not have money and did not seek to be rich.

I sought God's face for direction. I found myself asking the question, how can I best use what God has given me to continue the conservative view of the Drive of Faith in training the unfortunate who could not (for one reason or another) attend a resident college? At that moment I felt an anointing of the Holy Spirit to offer a college education online or correspondence to any serious-minded believer at a cost anyone could afford ($1 a lesson to cover postage and incidentals). It was to be a college that did not give a diploma or degrees, a college education that was not in competition with any other school. We were glad to find that other colleges accepted our credits after we started.

The name I gave it was *Pentecostal Conservative School of the Bible*. This was an education in Pentecostal conservatism, conservatism to the core. It proclaimed Pentecostal truth as it was originally believed by the patriots of our Pentecostal heritage. It was an education with the Bible as its textbook. This was another challenge as I neared the end of a life devoted to the *Drive of Faith*.

Most of the first one hundred applicants quit after a month or two when they discovered it was on the college level, not oversized Sunday school lessons. I made it clear from the beginning that this education was not for everyone; it takes real concentrated effort to take lessons outside the classroom and most people do not have that kind of ambition. For several years a number of students finished one or more of the dozen courses I have written. Only one person has finished every lesson. The courses involved over 1,000 sets of questions, 1,000 memory verses, and reading the Bible Book in each course twice. That student is now waiting for me to finish a course in 1 and 2 Corinthians.

Several incarcerated believers took my courses. Some of those were saved and one was filled with the Holy Spirit in prison. After ten or twelve years I began to realize that without adequate help from someone close by, I would not be able to continue the correspondence lessons. They took hours to correct and properly deal with and I was not about to give anyone a diluted education. I do not take any on line students now unless I get a request from a pastor who assures me the student is serious. I do not enjoy giving time and effort to someone who is going to quit halfway through. I am sure my readers understand that.

How does one close a book like this? When my editor read this last statement she felt inspired to write the following that I am honored to add as the closing remarks to the *Drive of Faith:*

> *It has been a journey through several decades and as many states over your lifetime. The journey has all the markers of an adventure. You have taken risks, read the roadmap, made turns, changed direction and committed yourself to the outcomes and consequences that resulted from every choice. You have negotiated curves, climbed difficult grades, picked up passengers and even coasted on fumes at times. In all of this you have followed a Guide who was ever beside you, always inside you, and knew the path that you took. Your turn behind the wheel nears its end. Throughout the trip you have learned many things. You have grown as a man and as a leader. Even now, though going at a less reckless speed, you have not pulled your keys from the ignition, but continue to follow the Divine compass as you share your vision of the journey with every one who cares to know. You guide others who follow their own similar path. And your eye is still on the roadmap; you have not lost sight of the goal. You remain ever a mile marker for others.*

> *By Dr. Dawn Coffin, MLS, DD*

CPSIA information can be obtained
at www.ICGtesting.com
Printed in the USA
FSHW020539261119
64514FS